ROUTLEDGE LIBRARY EDITIONS:
AGRIBUSINESS AND LAND USE

Volume 14

THE COMMON AGRICULTURAL POLICY

T0271330

THE COMMON AGRICULTURAL POLICY

Past, Present and Future

BRIAN E. HILL

LONDON AND NEW YORK

First published in 1984 by Methuen & Co. Ltd

This edition first published in 2024
by Routledge
4 Park Square, Milton Park, Abingdon, Oxon OX14 4RN

and by Routledge
605 Third Avenue, New York, NY 10158

*Routledge is an imprint of the Taylor & Francis Group, an informa
business*

British Library Cataloguing in Publication Data
A catalogue record for this book is available from the British
Library

ISBN: 978-1-032-48321-4 (Set)
ISBN: 978-1-032-46700-9 (Volume 14) (hbk)
ISBN: 978-1-032-46776-4 (Volume 14) (pbk)
ISBN: 978-1-003-38321-5 (Volume 14) (ebk)

DOI: 10.4324/9781003383215

Publisher's Note
The publisher has gone to great lengths to ensure the quality of this
reprint but points out that some imperfections in the original copies
may be apparent.

Disclaimer
The publisher has made every effort to trace copyright holders and
would welcome correspondence from those they have been unable
to trace.

The Common Agricultural Policy
Past, present and future

BRIAN E. HILL

METHUEN
LONDON AND NEW YORK

First published in 1984 by
Methuen & Co. Ltd
11 New Fetter Lane, London EC4P 4EE

Published in the USA by
Methuen & Co.
in association with Methuen, Inc.
733 Third Avenue, New York, NY 10017

© 1984 Brian E. Hill

Printed in Great Britain at the
University Press, Cambridge

British Library Cataloguing in Publication Data
Hill, Brian E.
    The common agricultural policy, past, present and
future. – (Methuen EEC series)
    1. Agriculture and state – European Economic
Community countries
    I. Title
    338.1'81   HD1920.5.Z8

    ISBN 0-416-32180-1
    ISBN 0-416-32190-9 Pbk

Library of Congress Cataloging in Publication Data
Hill, Brian E.
    The common agricultural policy.

    (The Methuen EEC series)
    Bibliography: p.
    Includes index.
    1. Agriculture and state – European Economic Community
countries. 2. Agricultural price supports – European
Economic Community countries. 3. Surplus agricultural
commodities – European Economic Community countries.
4. Agriculture – Economic aspects – European Economic
Community countries. I. Title. II. Series.
    HD1920.5.Z8H55 1984   338.1'81'094   84-4556
    ISBN 0-416-32180-1
    ISBN 0-416-32190-9 (pbk.)

Contents

Abbreviations

AUA	Agricultural Unit of Account
CAP	Common Agricultural Policy
EAEC	European Atomic Energy Commission
EC	European Community(ies)
ECC	European Communities Commission
ECSC	European Coal and Steel Community
ECU	European Currency Unit
EEC	European Economic Community
EFTA	European Free Trade Association
EMS	European Monetary System
EMU	Economic and Monetary Union
EUA	European Unit of Account
FEOGA	European Agricultural Guarantee and Guidance Fund (the abbreviation comprises the initials of its French title)
GATT	General Agreement on Tariffs and Trade
GNP	Gross National Product
MCA	Monetary Compensatory Amount
OECD	Organization for European Co-operation and Development
SMP	Skim Milk Powder
UA	Unit of Account
VAT	Value Added Tax

Figures and tables

General editor's preface

The European Economic Community came into existence on 1 January 1958, having formally been established by the signature of the Treaty of Rome on 25 March 1957 and by its subsequent ratification by the governments of the original six member states. The Rome Treaty also established the European Atomic Energy Community (Euratom), and the European Coal and Steel Industry had been created in 1952 by the Treaty of Paris. These bodies, united since 1967 under a common Council and with a Common Commission and generally known as the EEC or the European Communities, are a powerful and complex force, affecting the lives of the citizens of all member states and the economies and policies of many non-member states.

Since 1958 many of the main policy objectives of the Rome (and the Paris) Treaty have been realized. There remain, however, policy areas where progress has been very slow and difficult, and on the whole it is these problems that draw attention and criticism. There is no doubt that the member states and sectoral interest groups of the enlarged and enlarging Community are still experiencing considerable difficulty in reaching an acceptable balance between national and Community interest, a situation that is not greatly assisted by the low level of general interest in the populace at large of the character, aims and procedures of the Community and its institutions.

The more widespread dissemination of information and opinion about the Community deserves higher priority than has hitherto been given. This series of books, in consequence, is designed to cater for the needs of both those with more specialist interests and those with a more general desire for ready access to fact and informed opinion. Each book is written by an expert on the particular subject, yet with a style and structure that will make it accessible to the non-specialist. The series is designed to facilitate the crossing of disciplinary boundaries and hence to encourage discussion and debate in a multi-disciplinary context (in the field of European Studies, for example) of one of the most powerful and dynamic communities in the world.

R. A. Butlin
Loughborough University of Technology

Author's preface

Throughout its first quarter of a century (1958–83) the European Community appears to have been dominated by agriculture. The Common Agricultural Policy is the major common policy, regarded as central and essential to the Community by many 'Eurocrats'. It has taken, and still takes, a massive share of the Community's annual budget. Yet it is understood by few people. Perhaps this is not surprising since the public view of the policy is that it expensively subsidizes the production of more food than we can eat and sells the surpluses to other countries at low prices. These incredible facts are naturally confusing but they are not the whole story – the complex details are far worse than is generally realized!

It is virtually impossible to appreciate what is happening in the CAP without examining its origins. I have therefore started the story by explaining why agriculture is regarded as an economic and social problem area by all governments. After a brief consideration of the different agricultural policies adopted by various European countries before the days of the Community, attention is then focused upon the latter's formation and the economic and political framework within which its agricultural policy developed. The birth and development of the policy are shown to be natural extensions of the policies previously existing in the dominant countries of the original six members of the Community. This 'past' section of the book ends by describing the first enlargement of the Community in 1973 to include Denmark, Ireland and the UK.

In the 'present' section of the book are analysed the problems of the CAP as it operates today. Successive chapters deal with the monetary problems arising from the 'green' currency system, the expensive generation and costly disposal of surpluses and the internationally inequitable methods by which the policy is financed. A final chapter in this section appraises the policy in terms of the achievement of its objectives, showing that by this criterion the policy is remarkably unsuccessful despite its high costs.

Throughout its existence the CAP has been the subject of much criticism and many reform proposals. The opening chapter of the 'future' section analyses the major reform proposals not only in terms of their economic and social consequences but also their political acceptability. Finally, the consequences of further enlargement of the Community are considered. Greece acceded in 1981, too recently for its effects to be obvious, and it is therefore discussed alongside the potential accessions of Portugal and Spain.

Recognizing the importance of this subject to anyone studying the European Community I have carefully avoided any technical jargon. The book should therefore be suitable for students and others from a wide variety of disciplines. In case the tone of this preface should seem too dismal, perhaps I might at this point admit to a conclusion which gives reason for hope, if not optimism – that although the fundamentals of the 'agricultural problem' will be with us forever, the policy for dealing with it can be greatly improved both in terms of lower costs and greater effectiveness.

Brian E. Hill
University of Nottingham

Acknowledgements

Any book of this nature of necessity owes much to many others whose works, in agricultural economics in general or on European agriculture in particular, have helped to shape my thoughts. My thanks are due to them in addition to the authors who have been specifically acknowledged in the text. I have been fortunate in having my typescript constructively criticized by two people – Professor Robin Butlin of Loughborough University, the series editor, and my Nottingham colleague Professor Tony Rayner. Their suggestions have been gratefully received, but despite their efforts there doubtless remain many imperfections for which I must claim responsibility. Finally I must thank my wife for typing this book from a manuscript which would certainly have defeated anyone else.

Introduction

The Common Agricultural Policy (CAP) is basically a collection of economic measures whose justification is both economic and social. In discussing and analysing the CAP we concentrate on the socio-economic nature of the problems of agriculture and of the policies for their amelioration. It is as well here to note the framework within which these comments are applied, in particular the political, economic and cultural philosophy. The prevailing values of West European society are to be assumed in all that follows. With Pigou, we hold that the objective of Man is not the pursuit of wealth as such but 'welfare', a broader concept – thus the socio-political objectives of governments include not only the achievement of an abundance of goods and services but also a reasonably equitable distribution of a stable national income. 'Welfare' in our political system includes the legitimate desires of men in living happily – which requires more than the satisfaction of material needs: taking account of the need for security, the right to possess some property and sufficient independence to decide for themselves what work they wish to do. Our system regards the family as a basic economic unit, able to possess and hand on property and business assets.

Agriculture is man's oldest organized economic activity. In this analysis the framework is to some extent historical, emphasizing the constancy of change and tracing the current and future continuation of past forces. The book may be divided into three sections: Past, CAP Present and CAP Future. The 'Past' section begins by discussing the role of agriculture in economic development, noting how agriculture is itself transformed (Chapter 1). This is a recurrent topic which runs through the book as a unifying theme. In Chapter 2 a brief description of the common agricultural heritage of Europe's medieval past is given. Diverse emergences from this peasant period are shown to be at the root of the very different agricultures of the Community's present members. Chaper 3 sketches the troubled political and economic situations from which the Community of Six was born with the determination to unite for peace and prosperity. Agriculture's part in this process and the birth and development of the Common Agricultural Policy are considered in some detail. Finally, this section examines the first enlargement of the Community. Appendices to this chapter summarize the institutional and policy instruments of the CAP; they are situated here both to provide the details often referred to in Chapter 3 and also to act as a simple factual *aide mémoire* for the analyses of the following 'CAP Present' section.

In the first three chapters of the 'CAP Present' section (Chapters 4–6) critical examinations of the CAP as it has operated and is still operating are presented. These examine the CAP's monetary, surplus and cost problems in turn. The findings are expanded in Chapter 7 which appraises the policy in terms of the achievement of its objectives.

The 'CAP Future' section consists of two chapters. Chapter 8 considers a wide variety of reform proposals. In Chapter 9 (the concluding chapter of the book), the prospects for changing the CAP in the future are speculated upon. One obvious incentive is the second enlargement of the Community, already begun with the accession of Greece in 1981. Readers who persist to the end will have discovered that politicians have nurtured the CAP for social and political reasons in defiance of historical economic forces. Such readers will not be surprised that no ideal solution has been found, or exists, for the ills of agriculture. The author believes firmly, however, that amelioration is both possible and highly desirable; if this admittedly personal interpretation of the CAP helps in any way towards an understanding which is quintessential to progress it will have been worthwhile.

1 Agriculture and economic development

Agriculture is the major economic activity of primitive societies; in the countries of the Third World today it accounts for typically half to three-quarters of the economically active population. In Western Europe this proportion is much lower, indeed for most developed countries the figure is less than 10 per cent; in some it is very much lower. The relative decline in agriculture as economies develop is so characteristic that the proportion of the population employed in agriculture is frequently used as a measure of the level of development achieved. This chapter is concerned with the interrelationships between agriculture and economic development. The aspect is to some extent historical, but not entirely so, for the processes which are examined have by no means finished even in Europe. Their continuation here is helping to shape the future as they have the past. Their continuation in the Third World is, through trading links, also of considerable significance to Western Europe.

Before investigating the role of agriculture in economic development it is as well to consider what is meant by this term. The classical notion of economic development is that the discovery of a new production method causes output to increase and this permits, indeed induces, a corresponding increase in population so that income per head returns to its prior level. This is the view which was popularized by Malthus in particular. Such economic development is largely an increase in numbers without the individual members of society being better off in any real sense. For there to be an improvement in social welfare as a result of economic development there must be an increase in income per head. In practice, population growth is generally associated with the process. Thus, Kuznets, the modern pioneer in this field, defines economic development (though preferring to call it economic growth) as 'a sustained increase in a nation's total and *per capita* product, most often accompanied by a sustained and significant rise in population' (quoted in Metcalf 1969, 72). The word 'sustained' is important: history can provide many instances of temporary developments which have collapsed. It may be that the distribution of income is as important as the average level, for a raised average income can be either a raised income for the majority or a very high income for a minority, with the majority no better off than before. The latter could be the situation where ruling minorities dissipate their raised incomes in activities to defend their ruling positions or to enhance their social positions, without their country's economic capacity to produce being further expanded. Thus did ancient civilizations spend their 'surplus' on great walls, pyramids, palaces and temples; their archaeological debris is magnificent, but the lot of their peasants must surely have been no better than if the growth in productive capacity utilized for great monuments had not occurred. It is probable that there can be no *sustained* development unless it benefits the majority of the society who provide the efforts by which progress is made.

In the light of the foregoing we could accept Kuznets's definition that economic development is a sustained increase in a nation's total and *per capita* product, but it is advisable to bear in mind the major implication. This is that, contrary to the classical view, production must *continually* outstrip population. As all societies were originally agricultural, the root of the process is an increase in agricultural productivity.

A pattern of economic development

It is instructive to analyse the process of economic development as a series of chronological steps starting with an isolated primitive society dominated by agriculture. In such a society the population is largely concerned with providing the three basic essentials of food, clothing and shelter. The peasants who produced food would at first also have made their own clothes, primarily from wool and animal skins, and built their own shelters. Later, their well-being would have been enhanced by specialization, with some becoming spinners and weavers, millers, smiths and carpenters, exchanging their services, at first directly and eventually through the use of money, for the food produced by their fellows. Schultz (1954, 32) has termed such an economy 'high food drain', referring to the fact that 75 per cent or more of income is spent on food. This is the prevailing situation examined by Richardo, Malthus and Mill and termed by them 'pre-industrial', which is misleading because it suggests an automatic movement towards industrialization. However, in this situation suppose that there is an increase in food production so that food producers, after satisfying their own needs, have a larger surplus to sell and so have higher real incomes. The extra food marketed must result in lower food prices and consequently in higher real incomes for people in the non-agricultural sector; this real income effect of lower food prices is considerable because – as already stated – a very high proportion of total income is spent on food. Raised incomes increase the effective demand for the non-food sector which consequently becomes more profitable; this in turn stimulates further investment which provides greater job opportunities. If the increase in agricultural output continues, there will be a continuing relative decline in food prices, implying higher real incomes for the non-agricultural sector. This will reduce the pressure to raise wages, thus maintaining profitability and investment. It must be emphasized that the initiation and continuation of this development requires food output to expand more rapidly than population, resulting in an increase in *per capita* incomes.

Before any development occurs, the villages contain both food producers and craftsmen. Increased food production relative to population, through the process outlined above, expands the number and in time the variety of craftsmen. These cottage industries are important because they familiarize a significant proportion of the population, including many in the agricultural sector, with non-agricultural skills. The scene is now set for industrialization: economies of scale are such that larger firms have much lower costs of production than cottage industries. Their labour productivity in particular is considerably greater, so that cottage producers, being uncompetitive, become an appropriate labour input to factories. The greater output of goods reduces prices, so that aided by falling food prices the demand for non-food goods is strong and expanding.

Factories produce capital goods as well as consumer goods. Agriculture, accounting at this stage of development for the bulk of the population, is the major market for both, and is itself improved by the capital goods purchased. An increasing variety of better tools enhance labour productivity – scythes replace sickles, steel-tipped ploughshares take the place of iron ones, and later, specialized machinery such as seed drills are introduced and powered machines substituted for horse and man power. These industrial inputs enable further increases in food production to occur. There is thus a major interaction between agriculture and industry, whereby the former provides food at declining prices and an expanding market for industrial products, whilst industrial inputs improve agricultural output; it is not surprising that this has been termed the 'virtuous circle' of development.

Typically, the enhanced food supply does lead to population growth. At first the number of people occupied in agriculture expands, although not as rapidly as numbers in the non-agricultural sector, which grows partly through a transfer of labour from agriculture as well as by multiplication. Eventually, the rate of migration from the agricultural to the industrial sector exceeds the former's population growth. So, in terms of employment, agriculture at first expands in absolute terms although declining relative to the remainder of the economy, then later it employs a declining number as well as a declining share of the population. Clearly agriculture contributes not only increased food supplies to economic development but is also initially the major source of labour.

The increasing interchange of goods and services between agriculture and industry implies a growing need for markets and better communications. This is underlined by the fact that industrial developments are largely urban and therefore geographically separate from agriculture. This separation encourages the development of processing, packaging, distributive and financial sectors.

At the beginning of this analysis we were dealing with a 'high food drain' economy with 75 per cent or more of income spent on food. Clearly the pace of development was greatly affected by the harvest. In time, as food prices fell relative to other goods, the proportion of income spent on food declined: still using Schultz's terminology the economy became 'intermediate food drain', where over 25 per cent but less than 75 per cent of income is spent on food. Such an economy is still considerably influenced by the food supply, but the vagaries of harvests are more likely to be modified through trade with neighbouring regions and countries. Finally, in the later stages of development the proportion of income spent on food falls below 25 per cent – 'low food drain' – and the population is largely independent of agriculture.

Return to agricultural resources

In the simple pattern of economic development outlined above, it is clear that agriculture plays a fundamental role. It is now proposed to consider the effects of development upon agriculture itself.

Ernst Engel was a nineteenth-century German statistician who used data from his many observations to formulate a number of 'economic laws'. Today, whilst most of these 'laws' have failed to stand the test of time, one relationship is still accepted and is known as Engel's Law. It states that as income rises the proportion spent on food declines. Figures 1.1(a) and 1.1(b) represent this relationship in two ways. In 1.1(a) the relationship is drawn as stated. It has been redrawn as 1.1(b) to make clear that the total expenditure on food continues to rise as income increases, but at a decreasing rate. At low incomes people spend most of their income on food just to try to get enough to fill them; as income rises they can soon eat no more in quantity but spend more by buying better-quality food. Figure 1.1(a) also indicates as a corollary of Engel's Law that, assuming for simplicity that all income is spent, expenditure on non-food items takes an increasing share of total expenditure. Hence, as economic development occurs and incomes rise, the non-agricultural sector must grow more rapidly than the agricultural sector. Though the latter may grow in *absolute* terms it suffers a *relative* decline.

The more rapid growth of the non-agricultural sector means that employment is increasing there. In agriculture, employment may increase or decrease, depending on the rate of improvement in labour productivity. Either way, the more rapid growth of the non-agricultural sector means that the demand for labour is greater than in agriculture. Higher wages then attract labour from agriculture, so the economic mechanism by which labour is 'released' from the land

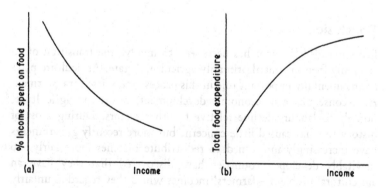

Figures 1.1 (a) and 1.1 (b) Engel's Law: the *proportion* of income spent on food declines as income rises; this is shown (a) and redrawn in (b) to show that total food expenditure increases at a declining rate as income increases.

results in higher incomes outside agriculture than within. Because economic development in Europe has been continuous but labour is slow to adjust to income differences by changing occupations, there is a persistent excess of labour in agriculture resulting in relatively low incomes.

Agricultural production is peculiarly subject to natural influences – the weather and the incidence of pests and diseases. These very variable factors cause the quantity of output to fluctuate unpredictably and uncontrollably. Revenues from the sale of output also fluctuate in consequence. Production costs, however, are much more stable: when the land is ploughed and the seed sown, the harvest is unknown; only the costs of harvesting vary with the yield. As profit is the difference between a variable revenue and a relatively stable cost it must itself be variable, and so therefore are the farmers' incomes based on such profits. Incomes in agriculture are thus variable as well as being low.

The discussion has centred on the returns to labour but could be extended to other resources. Thus the growth of land productivity in the form of higher yields reduces its relative returns. Unlike labour, land is physically fixed so that only particular pieces of land – usually on the urban fringe – can leave agriculture for more highly paid uses. Other resources, such as buildings, machinery and livestock, wear out or can be sold so that their employment can be adjusted to their returns. Agricultural land and labour suffer persistently low relative returns because the former is geographically immobile and the latter is occupationally immobile, as the skills and life-style peculiar to agriculture hinder transfer to other sectors.

Conclusion

Economic development has been seen to involve the transition of an economy from its initial primarily agricultural state. Agriculture plays a fundamentally important role in this process and is itself transformed. As a consequence of economic development, returns in agriculture, notably to labour, decline relative to other sectors. During most of history this has caused little concern, but more recently governments have increasingly intervened to redistribute incomes more fairly. So inevitably developed countries have discovered that they have an agricultural problem – farmers' incomes which they regard as unfairly low – and they have therefore introduced a variety of policies to deal with this problem.

2 The development of modern agriculture: problems and policies

Ancient agricultural practices and their associated political and social systems were basically similar over much of Europe. Despite these common beginnings and the universality of the forces of economic development, the agricultures of European countries were remarkably diverse by the twentieth century. This chapter can only hint at the historical forces responsible for this situation, leaving the interested reader to pursue the topic elsewhere. The focus of attention here is the agricultural problems which history and economic development have bequeathed to this century and the nature of the policies to which they gave rise before the European Community came into being.

Open fields

In medieval Europe cultivation was generally based on the open-field system, so called because the very large fields involved were not subdivided by hedges or fences. They were, however, subdivided into many separate plots, with each peasant cultivating a number of plots allocated annually by lot and therefore widely scattered. The peasants and open fields were in the immediate control of lords of the manor. This system persisted for centuries, breaking up in a variety of ways. Britain illustrates one extreme in which the lords of the manor ultimately became landlords, turning the open fields into large farms, with the peasants becoming variously tenant farmers, landless labourers or vagrants. At the other extreme, the peasants became the landowners and so the farms they possessed were typically small and composed of a multitude of small separate plots, these being their scattered plots from the open fields. This latter situation applied to much of continental Europe as a consequence of peasant revolts. In some parts nobles succeeded in maintaining their estates or regaining parts of them after revolutions, so that small fragmented 'peasant' farms and larger farms may exist side by side.

Table 2.1 The number and size of farms over 1 hectare in the EC, 1977

	Number (000)	Average area (ha)	No. of parcels [†]
Germany	859	14.4	11
France	1149	25.5	18
Italy	2192	7.4	11
Netherlands	137	15.0	4
Belgium	99	14.5	6
Luxembourg	5	25.4	15
UK	262	65.6	(1)
Ireland	225	22.5	(1)
Denmark	116	23.5	(1)
Greece	732	4.3	7
EC 10	5784	15.5	—
Portugal (1968)	500	8.6	6
Spain (1972)	1932	14.9	14

Sources: ECC (1982a), 290; OECD (1973); OECD (1974a); OECD (1975); Rickard (1970)

Note: [†] Fragmentation data in Six relate to *circa* 1970

Table 2.1 gives some structural characteristics of West European farms. British farms are seen to be much larger than elsewhere, reflecting their different emergence from the open fields. Nevertheless British farms are on average too small to benefit fully from the available economies of size which modern production methods entail. To achieve minimum average costs of production farms need to have 150 to 200 hectares. So it can be seen that Community agriculture has a very outdated size-structure. Generalizations frequently hide much truth, so in this case Table 2.2 provides further structural information and reveals a very important paradox. This is that most farms are small, but most land belongs to large farms. Much of the total agricultural area is farmed in units which are large enough to be efficient whilst the remaining land is subdivided into many small and therefore inherently inefficient farms.

Protection

The nineteenth century saw the establishment of large farms across the lands of the 'new world', including the prairies of North America. In

Table 2.2 The distribution of farms and land by farm size, EC, 1980

per cent

Farm size (ha)	Germany		France		Italy[+]		Netherlands		Belgium		Luxembourg		UK		Ireland[+]		Denmark		Greece[+]	
	Farms	Land	Farms	Land	Farms	Land	Farms	Land	Farms	Land	Farms	Land	Farms	Land	Farms	Land	Farms	Land	Farms	Land
1–<5	32	5	21	2	68	22	24	4	29	5	19	2	12	2	15	1	11	2	71	39
5–<10	19	9	15	4	17	16	20	10	20	9	11	3	12	3	17	1	18	6	21	30
10–<20	23	22	21	12	8	15	29	27	26	25	14	8	16	8	30	3	26	19	7	18
20–<50	22	44	30	38	4	17	24	45	21	40	38	48	27	27	30	13	35	40	2	10
≥50	4	20	13	43	2	30	3	15	4	21	17	40	33	60	9	82	10	33	0	3
	100	100	100	99	99	100	100	101	100	100	99	101	100	100	101	100	100	100	101	100

Source: Derived from ECC (1982a), 290–1

Notes: [+]1977

Percentages have been rounded to the nearest whole number and may therefore not sum to 100 the middle of the century the development of railways across the prairies and steamships across the Atlantic gradually reduced the cost of transporting wheat to Europe. Eventually, wheat could be landed in European ports at prices much lower than those previously ruling in Europe. In the 1870s American grain began to arrive in large quantities; few of the relatively small and inefficient European producers could compete, and they began to demand protection. The last twenty years of the century were termed 'the Great Depression', a recession which affected all sectors. Accordingly many countries adopted high tariffs during these years to protect both agriculture and industry from imports. The UK remained the only major country to adhere to the principles of free trade. Despite the flood of cheap American grain, farmers received no protection and the arable areas of the east and south of the country were severely depressed.

Livestock producers were affected much less by foreign competition than were the grain producers. Transport developments included refrigeration in ships, so that meat arrived in Europe from Australasia and America. The growth in imports was less spectacular than for grain, and the market for meat was expanding as living standards improved. Also, cheap grain meant cheap feed for many types of livestock. Clearly the interests of grain and livestock producers were opposed. The adoption by many countries of tariffs to protect home grain producers against imports probably reflected the relative political influences of the two types of producers rather than any natural agricultural interest as a whole. Grain producers tended to have the larger farms, to be better educated and organized, and so able to make their views known. Livestock were more the province of the smallholders who had until recently been peasants and whose opinions were unheard as much as unheeded.

Denmark and the Netherlands stand out as being more far-sighted than most of their neighbours. In these two countries free trade continued to flourish, with agriculture becoming to some extent a processing industry, turning cheap imported feeding stuffs into meat to be exported to surrounding industrializing areas.

The next major change in the fortunes of agriculture came with the end of the First World War. The agriculture of large areas was devastated, so that European food production was low and prices high; tariffs were reduced to low levels or removed altogether. With the recovery of output prices fell sharply in 1921, the fall being exacerbated by general economic recession. This situation continued, with minor fluctuations, until conditions worsened markedly in the depression of the early 1930s. Once more, grain prices took the brunt of the price collapse and tariffs, reintroduced during the 1920s, were substantially increased. In the 1930s most of Europe was vigorously pursuing 'beggar-my-neighbour' policies which sought to protect employment at home by preventing imports and at the same time to improve the domestic economy by expanding exports. Needless to say, these policies did not work; indeed they made a bad situation worse.

Between the late 1920s and early 1930s agricultural import tariffs increased greatly. To make sure that they achieved their objective of reducing imports the latter were in many cases also limited by quota. Even those countries dedicated to free trade were forced to intervene to try to save their agricultures from irrational cut-throat competition. The Netherlands and Denmark attempted to improve quality to maintain exports but also found it necessary to protect and subsidize domestic producers. In the UK free trade had given way to Imperial Preference – not the abandonment of free trade so much as its restriction to the Empire. Essentially this meant the export of British manufactures to the Empire and the import of Empire products; since these were to a considerable extent agricultural, British agriculture remained virtually unprotected. However, the farmers were encouraged to help themselves via marketing boards, which by controlling supplies could raise prices to consumers.

Government intervention

It is evident that during the late nineteenth and the twentieth centuries European governments intervened in agriculture to an increasing extent. The next few pages will briefly explore the reasons for intervention and the main methods used.

REASONS FOR INTERVENTION

Economic efficiency. Free economies have long been recognized to be prone to alternate booms and depressions; much government activity has been concerned to smooth this tendency. In agriculture, super-imposed upon the ups and downs of the business cycle are violent price fluctuations due to the influence of the weather, pests and diseases. These unpredictable factors cause output to vary substantially from season to season, but consumers always want to eat the same quantity of food. So gluts cause dramatic price collapses and minor shortages persuade prices to soar. Clearly, this inherent instability of agricultural prices is confusing to farmers who are unable to discern consumer requirements amid such chaotic price changes and are therefore unable to plan and invest sensibly. Hence, government intervention to stabilize agricultural prices has become accepted as a standard requirement of agricultural policy.

Production efficiency requires not only stable prices but also the application of modern production techniques. For the former, education and research is necessary, but an industry composed of hundreds of thousands of small independent producers is unable to organize such activities itself. These are normally, therefore, an area of government activity. As noted earlier, the structure of much of European agriculture is obsolete. Modern production techniques, particularly those involving large items of expensive machinery, are hardly suited to small fragmented farms. Consequently most governments have introduced measures to encourage the consolidation of farms – generally by the exchange of scattered fragments with neighbours and the amalgamation of small farms to produce larger ones.

Security of food supply. This strategic argument is that a country must produce enough of its own food supply to ensure that it can maintain its population when imports are prevented by war. Hence, agriculture must not be allowed to decline in the face of foreign competition. A supplementary argument, common in the past, was that agricultural support ensured a large rural population which was potentially a major source of soldiers in the event of a war.

Equity. In the twentieth century it is generally considered unfair that some sectors of society should enjoy incomes which are much lower than elsewhere. As argued in the previous chapter, economic development naturally results in relatively low returns to agricultural resources, especially labour. This social motive for government intervention has become increasingly important until in the post Second World War period it has become the primary consideration.

Reasonable food prices. This phrase is used here because it is currently in vogue although it is not capable of objective definition. In the UK it means cheap food for consumers, an important policy objective since the Corn Laws were repealed in 1846. For most other European countries consumers' interests have tended to be subservient to those of producers. Clearly, what is reasonable is a subjective opinion. Despite its vagueness – or perhaps because of it – this phrase occurs frequently in government statements, and it will be discovered later amongst the objectives of the European Community.

Political. Farmers tend to be rather vociferous. Their organizations are effective lobbying bodies because of the large numbers of voters which they represent. Also it is likely that political ears are particularly receptive to farmers' arguments since an undue proportion of politicians are themselves farmers or landowners.

Conservation. Recent years have seen a growing appreciation of the importance of agriculture in relation to the environment. This aspect of agriculture has been little heeded in the past but is likely to become of more importance in the future.

METHODS OF INTERVENTION

It is not proposed to attempt a comprehensive analysis of the methods by which governments intervene in agriculture; interested readers should consult standard agricultural economics textbooks. It was noted above that the primary objective was to raise the incomes of the agricultural population on equity grounds. In the past this has been attempted through raising agricultural prices above their free market levels. Two basic methods exist by which this may be achieved. First, the supply of agricultural products may be curtailed, thus forcing up their prices. A reduction of supplies may be achieved by a considerable variety of measures including quota restrictions on domestic producers or imports, tariff restriction of imports, and the export of some supplies with the aid of subsidies. Second, production and trade may be allowed to determine output and prices with the consequence that the latter will be 'too low', so that farmers have to be compensated for low prices by being given government subsidies. This, termed the deficiency payments method of support (since the deficiency between market and 'fair' prices was made up by the government) was the method used in the UK in the post-war period until accession to the EEC. It meant that consumers received food at low prices and taxpayers paid for the policy. In contrast, policies which curtail supplies by any means whatever raise prices to consumers. Both deficiency payments and supply-reducing policies raise prices to farmers and therefore retain resources within agriculture which would otherwise leave.

The economic and social conflict

Economic development leads to the relative decline of agriculture and of agricultural earnings. History has left Europe a legacy of small fragmented inefficient farms. Clearly, to encourage labour resources to leave agriculture, enabling its structure to improve, incomes *should* be relatively low. But low incomes are socially unacceptable. The agricultural policies of this century are fundamentally social in that their primary objective is to raise incomes. They therefore diametrically oppose the economic forces of history. It is the struggle of Western Europe attempting to reconcile the irreconcilable to which the remainder of this book is devoted.

3 The development of the Common Agricultural Policy

This chapter begins with a brief digression from its agricultural theme to explain the movement towards European integration which provided the framework within which the Common Agricultural Policy (CAP) was to develop. It then proceeds to examine the first decade of the European Economic Community (EEC), detailing the evolution of the CAP and its introduction into the member states. It was not to be expected that such a major international policy could be established easily, but, despite many problems, much was achieved. The second decade, for a variety of reasons to be discussed, proved unexpectedly difficult and in some ways the CAP came to be viewed by many as not so much an achievement as an intractable problem area. The chapter concludes with an account of the further difficulties caused by the enlargement of the Community to include three new members, one of which, the UK, soon decided that the terms upon which she had entered, particularly with respect to the CAP, were unfair and should be renegotiated.

West European integration

In the years immediately following the Second World War two distinctly different approaches to European unity became increasingly evident. The British and Scandinavians viewed European unity as intergovernmental co-operation, whilst France and some of her immediate neighbours desired a federalist system whereby international institutions would be created which would have some powers beyond the national sovereignties of member states. Although it had little supranational content, the first positive post-war movement in this latter direction was the formation of Benelux, a customs union, introduced on 1 January 1948 and composed of Belgium, the Netherlands and Luxembourg. In May 1948 a European Congress held at The

Hague adopted a resolution calling for progress towards economic and political union. Belgium and France proposed that a European parliamentary Assembly operating by majority vote should be created, but the British view that decisions should be by the unanimous agreement of governments prevailed. Consequently the Council of Europe, born in 1949 from the Congress, became largely a debating forum.

Coal and steel were the fundamental war materials of the Second World War; after the war Germany's supplies of these materials were controlled by the Allies through the International Ruhr Authority. The recovery of the German economy could not be complete without these basic means of production, yet handing back control was regarded as endangering the future peace of Europe. The Schuman Plan to solve this problem was put forward by France in 1950. The plan was to prevent national control of these materials by creating a common market in them controlled by a supranational authority. Thus each participating country would have equal access to these products; there would be no trade barrriers or discrimination of any kind between member states. Such a scheme appealed strongly to the federalists and was favoured by Germany not only for its economic benefits but also as a means of regaining international acceptance and respectability. In the event the European Coal and Steel Community (ECSC) was created in 1951 under the Treaty of Paris. Its members were France, West Germany, Italy and the Benelux countries; the UK had been invited to join but declined.

After several false starts towards further European unity the next major development was the result of an initiative from the Benelux countries. In 1955 they proposed the formation of a common market, to be concerned initially with economic integration but with the intention that as countries grew together economically they would ultimately move towards political unity. These ideas were accepted by the other members of the six states in the ECSC, who resolved to begin immediately to negotiate such a common market, establishing an inter-governmental committee under Paul-Henri Spaak for the purpose. The UK, having signed an 'Agreement of Association' with ECSC the previous year, was invited to participate. Initially she did so, but favoured the formation of a free trade area with no supranational elements, whereas the Six were determined on a full customs union including the creation of special international institutions. Consequently the UK soon withdrew, leaving the Six to continue their own negotiations. After considerable difficulties a Treaty was drawn up; it was signed in Rome in March 1957, establishing the European Economic Community (EEC) from 1 January 1958.

In 1956, whilst the Six proceeded with their negotiations in pursuit of economic and political unity, the UK proposed the creation of a free trade area covering much of Western Europe including the proposed customs union. The Six suspected that this was a ploy to ensure that their common market was still-born, and after complicated and lengthy negotiations the proposals were abandoned in 1958. Although they failed and the Six went their own way, these negotiations persuaded several other non-EEC countries that a free trade area would benefit their economies. They also felt that as individual states they were somewhat isolated by the introduction of the EEC. So early in 1959 negotiations were restarted. On 4 January 1960 the Stockholm Convention was signed forming the European Free Trade Association (EFTA). The signatories were Austria, Denmark, Norway, Portugal, Sweden, Switzerland and the UK. Europe was now at Sixes and Sevens. It should be noted that the EFTA dealt explicitly with industrial goods; agricultural goods were excluded.

In an abrupt about-turn, however, the UK decided that membership of the EEC would be in her interests. This change of heart reflected a growing realization that the UK was now in the second league of world powers, and the belief that she would be better off politically and economically in a united Europe. On 9 August 1961 Mr Macmillan gave formal notice to the EEC of the intention to negotiate for membership. Ireland, Denmark and Norway lodged their applications too. Agriculture was a particular problem and the lack of a defined policy within the Six presented a serious barrier to progress. Ultimately, President de Gaulle told a Press conference on 14 January 1963 that the UK was 'not ready' for membership. On 29 January negotiations were abruptly suspended at the request of the French.

The first decade of the EEC, 1958–67

ECONOMIC RATIONALE

The political background and motives for the formation of the EEC have been outlined above, and it is essential to bear in mind that the *primary* reason for the existence of the Community is political. In theory there should also be economic gains resulting from free trade within the Community. These gains are envisaged in Article 2 of the Treaty of Rome:

> The Community shall have as its task, by establishing a Common market and progressively approximating the economic policies of Member States, to promote throughout the Community a harmonious development of economic activities, a continuous and balanced expansion, an increase in stability, an accelerated raising of the standard of living and close relations between the States belonging to it.

The essential elements of a customs union and some of the common policies involved are outlined in Article 3:

> For the purposes set out in Article 2, the activities of the Community shall include, as provided in this Treaty and in accordance with the timetable set out therein
> (a) the elimination, as between Member States, of customs duties and of quantitative restrictions on the import and export of goods, and of all other measures having equivalent effect;
> (b) the establishment of a common customs tariff and of a common commercial policy towards third countries;
> (c) the abolition, as between Member States, of obstacles to freedom of movement for persons, services and capital;
> (d) the adoption of a common policy in the sphere of agriculture.

The article continues with a few other clauses listing other features which are of less import in the present context.

It must be noted that the clause relating to the adoption of a common agricultural policy follows immediately upon three clauses which are absolutely essential for the operation of a customs union. Is this because agriculture is of great importance, or is a common policy for it really essential? One consequence of the clauses establishing a common market is that commodities can be traded freely within this market, so that the only price differences which would persist are those which reflect transport costs. Thus food prices would find a common level, an essential feature of a customs union with its basis in free and fair trade because food prices are an important factor influencing wage demands and hence industrial costs. But each EEC member had its own previously existing agricultural policy, and the problems of this sector would continue to exist within the Community as they had in its constituent parts. So it was necessary to replace the individual policies with one common to the whole area.

OBJECTIVES OF THE CAP

Article 39 of the Treaty of Rome states that:

> The Common agricultural policy shall have as its objectives:
> (a) to increase agricultural productivity by promoting technical progress and by ensuring the rational development of agricultural production and the optimum utilisation of the factors of production, in particular, labour;
> (b) thus to ensure a fair standard of living for the agricultural community, in particular by increasing the individual earnings of persons engaged in agriculture;
> (c) to stabilise markets;
> (d) to assure the availability of supplies;
> (e) to ensure that supplies reach consumers at reasonable prices.

These objectives are paralleled by the agricultural policies of all the developed nations. They are for example very similar to the UK objectives as set out in the preamble to the 1947 Agriculture Act. The first objective of Article 39 relates to economic efficiency and is consistent with any government's general economic policy which is of course to seek efficiency in the use of national resources. It is the second objective which is at the heart of all agricultural policies – to provide a fair standard of living for the agricultural community. This and the following objective are aimed at the twin evils of agriculture – low and variable incomes. Finally the last two objectives have regard to the national security angle and consumer interests.

Several other Articles of the Treaty (38–47) deal specifically with agriculture, but they are vague compared to Article 39, generally saying what activities *may* be pursued in order to achieve the stated objectives. Thus the Treaty spells out the objectives but leaves open the question of what policy instruments should be introduced to achieve them.

INSTITUTIONAL ARRANGEMENTS

For the necessary development and co-ordination of economic policies the Treaty of Rome provided a number of administrative bodies. Chief among them are the Commission, the Council of Ministers and the

European Parliament (see Appendix 3.1). Community policies are implemented in the member states by their national parliaments and civil services. Before discussing the development of the CAP it is instructive to consider the decision-making process.

The Commission, situated in Brussels, is a body of professional civil servants, recruited from the member states but not representing their individual national interests. Its duties are to 'formulate recommendations or opinions in matters which are the subject of this Treaty ..., and to participate in the preparation of acts of the Council' (Article 155). Each major subject area with ministers in national governments has its own commissioner. It must be noted that the Commission has no powers of primary decision, although its regulations and directives designed to implement policy decisions are binding upon member states.

Decisions are taken by the Council of Ministers, each member state providing one member of its own government. Minor issues may be settled by majority voting. During the transitional period national interests were safeguarded by the unanimity principle when major issues were at stake, so each country could veto any development which appeared to be against its interests. It was intended that, later, all issues would be settled by majority voting; as will be seen, this was not to be.

The European Parliament was initially an Assembly whose members were appointed from national parliaments. It was essentially a debating institution meeting to receive the annual report of the Commission and having powers to question and discuss but not to take decisions. However, by carrying a motion of censure by a two-thirds majority it could force the resignation of the Commission as a body. This appointed Assembly was charged with the duty of drawing up 'proposals for election by direct universal suffrage' (Article 138). The Treaty does not express the hope of the more federalist-minded that a future elected Assembly would ultimately gain power at the expense of the Council of Ministers.

THE BIRTH AND DEVELOPMENT OF THE CAP

Before considering in detail how the policy was decided and introduced it is as well to summarize the conditions to which it was addressed. In 1958 over 15 million people – more than 20 per cent of the working population – were occupied in agriculture. The 6.5 million holdings were small and fragmented; despite existing national support policies, agricultural incomes were generally about half those in the non-agricultural sector. The geographical area of the Six included many differing climatic regions, varying from fertile lowlands, through less fertile hills and uplands to agriculturally inhospitable mountainous areas. Finally, in 1958 the different members of the Six had widely different policy instruments and attitudes, from relatively free trade in Italy to generous price supports and subsidies in Germany; whilst most price supports involved raising prices by restricting imports, Luxembourg had a system of deficiency payments. Clearly, forging a common agricultural policy to suit such diversity was a very formidable task.

The Treaty of Rome had envisaged a three-stage progression towards a common policy. In the first stage, for which three years were allotted, policies were to be formulated and agreed. In the second stage, to last until 1970, these policies were to be introduced. Finally, the last stage was to be the full operation of the policy in a unified market. Article 43 charged the Commission with the duty to study the existing situation in member states and then to propose a CAP which would achieve the objectives of Articles 39. As a beginning the Commission convened a conference at Stresa in July 1958, chaired by the first Commissioner for Agriculture, Dr Sicco Mansholt (previously the Netherlands Minister for Agriculture), and attended by the officials of national ministries and farmers' organizations. The conference emphasized wide differences of opinion between member states but produced an agreed set of objectives. These were (Butterwick and Rolfe 1968, 6-7):

(a) to increase agricultural trade within the Community and with other countries;
(b) to maintain a balance between structural and market policies;
(c) to avoid surpluses, and to give scope to the comparative advantages of the regions;
(d) to eliminate subsidies which would distort competition;
(e) to improve returns to capital and labour;
(f) to preserve the family structure of farming;
(g) to encourage rural industries which, by providing new job opportunities, would assist the removal of surplus labour, and to provide special aid to disadvantaged regions.

These aims were stated already in the Treaty of Rome but not so explicitly. One example is particularly interesting: the Treaty said that in working out a common agricultural policy due account should be taken of the social structure of agriculture, whilst (f) above interprets this to mean preserving the family structure of agriculture.

So the Treaty and the Conference had provided a list of not entirely compatible objectives, but to the Commission was delegated the task of proposing policy measures for their achievement. Early in 1960 their proposals were presented to the Assembly, as required under the Treaty, and eventually approved in June. By the end of the year the Council of Ministers had accepted the principal proposal, this being that internal agricultural prices should be raised to target levels by means of variable import levies. Thus community farmers would be protected from foreign competition and the lower prices prevailing on world markets.

Although the principles of the CAP had been agreed, the member states were reluctant to consider their application, clinging instead to their existing national policies. So 1961 saw little progress. although in June the Frence Prime Minister, M. Debré, declared that without a common agricultural policy there could be no common market. However, the first stage of the CAP had to be completed by the end of the year, this being the end of the three years allowed for policy formulation by the Treaty. Eventually the Council of Ministers met on 18 December to agree policy details before the deadline. Not surprisingly this proved to be impossible, and to comply with the deadline the clock was 'officially stopped' while negotiations proceeded day after day and through many nights. This celebrated Council marathon hammered out a package deal to be effective from midnight on 31 December 1961, although the final agreement was not concluded until 5.30 a.m. on 14 January 1962. This agreement initiated common policies for cereals, pigmeat, poultrymeat, eggs, fruit and vegetables, and wine, and outlined the method by which the policies were to be financed. It was followed by a second instalment concerning beef, veal, dairy products, and vegetable oils and fats in December 1963 after a second, though shorter, marathon.

TRANSITION TOWARDS COMMON PRICES

The ultimate goal was for common prices to rule throughout the community in accordance with the principles of a customs union. National prices were too disparate initially for member states to move immediately to common price levels because of the consequent disruption to production and markets. Nevertheless the free flow of trade in agricultural products within the Community could be achieved by compensating for these price differences when commodities crossed national frontiers. Thus if wheat was sold from France into Germany (low-price to high-price area) a border levy was used to raise the price from the French to the German level. Movements of wheat in the opposite direction were likewise permitted by using a subsidy to reduce its price when the wheat crossed the frontier. These *transitional compensatory amounts* were to be phased out gradually during the second stage of progression towards a full customs union: That is, national price levels were to be gradually aligned towards the common levels. Clearly, the major problem lay in deciding what the common prices were to be.

DETERMINATION OF COMMON PRICES

During the first two years of the CAP there was little progress in reducing the wide divergence between national prices. Early in 1964 the Commission therefore proposed that common price levels should be established for cereals, pigmeat, poultrymeat and eggs for the 1964/5 harvest year. Cereals were tackled first because they are the key product influencing all others, either because other products are converted from cereals (pigs and poultry eat a largely cereal diet) or because they compete with other products in terms of land use. The key price to be settled was that for soft wheat. This enjoyed a very much higher price in Germany than in France, with the other countries being somewhere in between. A low price would be a serious blow to German farmers and so politically difficult for their minister to accept; a high price would have been inflationary in France; no easy compromise could be found. Eventually, after the now traditional bargaining marathon of the Council in December 1964 common price levels were agreed, but the unified prices were not to come into force until 1 July 1967. Even this was well in advance of the date (31 December 1969) provided for in the Treaty. This accelerated progress was used to justify compensatory lump-sum payments to German farmers although in reality they were to sweeten the bitter pill of lower prices. It was also agreed to pay out of Community funds lump sums to Italy to compensate for the loss to livestock producers resulting from higher barley feed grain prices. Also, the importance of horticultural products to Italy was recognized by an undertaking to reconsider the common fruit and vegetables policy. This agreement is typical of the Council's package deals whereby the political or economic disadvantages to individual members resulting from the adoption of common measures are compensated by some particular and perhaps otherwise unrelated concession.

The target wheat price adopted represented lower prices for German, Italian and Luxembourg farmers, and higher prices for farmers in the other members states, much higher in the case of France. The target price was not, however, a weighted average of the previously ruling national prices, but instead comfortably exceeded this figure. Having fixed wheat prices at a high level, the prices of the other cereals, and of livestock products derived from them, had to be correspondingly high. This naturally caused an upward pressure on the prices of beef and dairy products negotiated later.

The December 1964 Council marathon fixed common prices for cereals, pig and poultry meats, and eggs, to be in force from 1 July 1967. Major disagreements, to be discussed below, prevented progress towards further price harmonization until 1966. Then, in July 1966, the Council of Ministers agreed prices for fruit and vegetables effective from 1 July 1967 and for the other major products, effective from 1 July 1968. As noted above, the high prices agreed for cereals necessarily set the tone for other products, and the Commission was forced to propose rather high price levels for beef and veal, milk and dairy products, sugar, olive oil and oil seeds. In the event the Council adopted even higher prices for milk, sugar, olive oil and oil seeds than those proposed by the Commission.

THE MECHANICS OF PRICE POLICY

This section outlines the principles of the policy; its details are more fully described in Appendix 3.2. Wheat is chosen to illustrate the system. A target price is fixed by the Council of Ministers, bearing in mind the objectives of Article 39, the proposals of the Commission and the arguments of the Economic and Social Committee. The target price relates to Duisberg, this being the main deficit area of the Community. Target prices in other regions are derived from it by the subtraction of transport costs. The target price is the level which the Community wishes to rule in the wholesale market. Because it is higher than prices in the world market some control over imports must be exercised. This takes the form of an import levy calculated as the difference between the import price and the port equivalent of the target price – the threshold price, approximately the target price less transport costs from the port. Thus the low-priced imported wheat is subject to a levy designed to ensure that it will at least equal the target price by the time it reaches wholesale markets. Clearly this system will keep prices above those on world markets as long as internal production is less than demand, but if internal supplies exceed consumption at the target price level, the price must fall even if foreign supplies were reduced to zero. To prevent internal surpluses of this nature depressing prices unduly, the Community arranges to purchase them at an intervention price set a few per cent below the target level. The intervention price is thus a minimum guaranteed price for producers. So long as surpluses are seasonal only, they can be purchased at the intervention price and stored; at other seasons, when reduced supplies cause prices to rise, the intervention stocks can be sold. Thus prices are stabilized as well as raised. If supplies chronically exceed consumption, intervention stores become full and some outlet has to be found. Clearly sales of these surpluses cannot take place internally without reducing the prices which the system is designed to protect. An external outlet is thus indicated, and surpluses are sold on the world market at world prices. This is made possible by giving exporters subsidies which enable them to trade at the lower world prices and still make a profit. Finally, if world prices rise above Community prices through some exceptional shortage, as happened briefly for some products in the commodity price boom of 1973/4, Community prices are held down through the imposition of export taxes equal to the difference between world and Community prices and thus rendering exports unprofitable.

The price support system outlined above applies to cereals, beef and veal, and milk. Variations of this system apply to most other products (described in Appendix 3.2). By the late 1970s about 95 per cent (by value) of Community produce was thus protected. For some other products two further systems are employed. *Additional product aid* provides variable subsidies which compensate for any shortfall between the Community's minimum prices and actual market prices (durum wheat, olive oil, rapeseed and tobacco). A *flat rate subsidy* is paid for a few minor products (cottonseed, flax, hemp, hops, silk-worms and dried grass).

PRICE POLICY, PROTECTION AND TRADE

In order to provide farmers with a 'fair' standard of living the prices of agricultural products were set well above world market levels. Agreements on prices were reached with great difficulty, as evidenced by the negotiating marathons noted earlier. It was politically easier for Ministers of Agriculture to agree to prices which raised rather than lowered their own national price levels. Thus, the prices which were set tended towards high levels. Consequently the Community became far more protectionist after the CAP was introduced than it, or its component states, had previously been. Table 3.1. underlines this point.

Table 3.1 EEC Import Protection before and after the CAP

	Level of protection per cent	
	Pre CAP (1959)	Post CAP (1968)
Live animals	14.4	48.5
Meat	19.0	52.1
Dairy produce	18.6	137.3
Cereals	13.5	72.4
Sugar	75.8	41.9

Source: Malgren and Scheckty (1969)

Article 110 of the Treaty of Rome states the intention of the Community to contribute 'to the harmonious development of world trade, the progressive abolition of restrictions on international exchanges and the lowering of customs barriers'. This evidently conflicts with its agricultural policy, and in striking a balance between its agricultural and trading policies the Community has inevitably favoured the former. Indeed, it is not unfair to say that for agricultural products the trading policy has been entirely dictated by domestic agricultural support policy.

STRUCTURAL POLICY

In the previous chapter the small and fragmented nature of most European farms and the historical forces which shaped them were discussed. This unfavourable structure of agriculture meant that production costs were high and incomes low, justifying the support of prices at very high levels. In the early 1960s when the principles of the prices policy were being determined, the Commission repeatedly emphasized that structural policies were also necessary. The individual member states already had their own structural policies, indeed these were frequently the major item of national expenditure on agriculture. Increasingly it was recognized that because structural change had output implications, a common price policy could be distorted by different national structural policies. As early as November 1960, the Council noted the need to co-ordinate national structural policies. Two years later the Commission proposed the establishment of a European Fund for Structural Improvement which would finance co-ordinated policies to improve the structural aspects of production, such as the consolidation of scattered plots into unified farms, the amalgamation of small farms and the provision of modern buildings. In 1963 the Council of Ministers rejected the proposed fund and instructed the Commission to revise its proposals so as to include the finance of structural measures by the newly established European Agricultural Guarantee and Guidance Fund (popularly known as FEOGA, the initials of its French title). The Commission's desire for a special structural fund but the Council's instruction to include the financing of such activities from the general fund, suggests a significant divergence of opinion on the relative importance of structural reform. Certainly the latter has taken second place in terms of Community-level action and expenditure.

FEOGA was established as part of the agreement initiating common policies which was finalized on 14 January 1962 after the first famous marathon. It was divided into two distinct sections: the Guarantee Section and the Guidance Section, designed to finance price and structural elements of policy respectively. The Guidance Section was primarily intended to contribute to the cost of projects designed to improve the marketing of agricultural produce: the provision of modern abbatoirs, grading and storage facilities, indeed anything which would improve the marketing channels used by farmers. Farm structural measures were added to this list when the proposed special fund was rejected. Early in 1964 it was agreed (Regulation EEC No. 17/64) to make Guidance Section grants of up to 25 per cent of the cost of approved projects. It was expected that these would absorb about a quarter of FEOGA expenditure and such disbursements were limited to one-third of Guarantee Section expenditures.

It was originally intended that national structural activities would be co-ordinated, eventually becoming Community-wide programmes. However, the difficulties attending the harmonization of measures designed to deal with problems in a wide variety of differing areas proved insurmountable, and the Guidance Section ended up helping to support approved but largely *ad hoc* projects. Consequently structural measures remained predominantly national, partly because they could thus be most easily tailored to suit local circumstances and partly because of the potential difficulties of the Community financing the vast expenditures which wider programmes would have necessitated.

Member states had each had their own legislation encouraging farm amalgamation since the early 1950s. Their activities had gradually extended to cover such things as modernization, irrigation, and helping groups and associations of producers. The latter were formed to strengthen the market power of farmers who individually were too small to strike good bargains in either buying or selling. There was also much expenditure of a more explicitly social nature providing the farming sector with retirement pensions, family allowances, and sickness and accident insurance. Whilst these measures helped to produce a more modern agricultural sector with rising productivity, they did nothing to cure the fundamental problems resulting from agriculture's sectoral decline in the course of economic development and the constant need to adjust by shedding labour. Indeed by ameliorating conditions within agriculture such policies tended to reduce the exodus of labour. However, it was gradually recognized that modernization and productivity increases were not sufficient by themselves to raise farm incomes and that the low-income problem was partly the result of agriculture's total income being subdivided amongst too many people.

FINANCING THE CAP

The principle of 'financial solidarity', i.e. that Common policies must be financed in common, is an important aspect of the Community. In order to finance the CAP the Community had to establish a central fund and decide on the methods of contribution by member states. As noted above, the fund, FEOGA, was established in January 1962 as part of the first marathon negotiating session spilling over from 1961 via the 'stopped clock' procedure. The following discussion relates initially to the Guarantee Section of the Fund.

Just as common prices were introduced stage by stage, so was common financing. In 1962/3 member states were reimbursed one-sixth of their guarantee expenditure, this proportion rising to 100 per cent on the introduction of the single market stage for cereals, pig and poultry meats and eggs on 1 July 1967.

FEOGA's source of revenue is a more complicated tale, often involving heated negotiations and alterations to the system as members sought to ensure that their contributions were not unduly heavy. In 1962/3 members' contributions to the Fund were determined by a percentage scale set out in Article 200. (Such scales are known in Community jargon as 'keys'. This and subsequent keys are detailed in Table Appendix 3.1.1.) In the following year 90 per cent of revenue was to be according to this key, the remaining 10 per cent to be contributed from agricultural import levies and duties and hence in proportion to each member's share of such imports. These two sources of revenue became 80 per cent and 20 per cent respectively for the next year.

The Council of Ministers, in the marathon negotiating session of December 1964, had agreed not only to introduce common prices for cereals from 1 July 1967 but to compensate Italy for the higher feeding stuff prices which would result. The form of compensation agreed was to redraft the fruit and vegetable policy proposals on more generous lines because of the importance of these products to Italy, and the limitation of Italy's contributions to FEOGA to 18 per cent and 22 per cent for the years 1965/6 and 1966/7 respectively (her contributions according to the fixed key would otherwise have been 28 per cent). This reduction of Italy's contributions implied higher contributions for other members, but neither these nor the long-term financing of FEOGA had been settled: the Commission was requested to formulate appropriate proposals.

FEOGA contributions posed a double problem for member states. First, they had to be allowed for when national budgets were drawn up and yet could not be either known or even planned. Second, the 'fixed' key contribution could be altered as they had been for Italy and so promised to become additional problems to aggravate the already difficult annual price negotiations. The Commission, mindful of these matters and being itself in favour of supranational developments, came up with a solution which dealt with all these points. In March 1965 it proposed that all national receipts from agricultural import levies and from the common external tariff on both agricultural and industrial goods should accrue directly to the Community.

Contributions would thus become automatic, not upsetting national budgets nor providing fuels for possibly acrimonious annual wrangles. To help it exercise its extended financial responsibility the Commission further proposed that the European Parliament should be given wider budgetary powers. The supranational content of this package was totally unacceptable to President de Gaulle. At the end of June France withdrew from all Community activities without even agreeing on an interim method of financing the CAP from 1 July. France's boycott has become known as the 'vacant chair' crisis.

This French reaction may seem rather extreme, but the principle involved is very important indeed. Under the 'qualified majority' system of voting in the Council of Ministers, France's objections to the sacrifice of sovereignty to the European Parliament which the proposals implied could have been overruled. She was not prepared to have sovereignty thus taken away. Eventually a settlement was reach in Luxembourg in January 1966. Under this 'Luxembourg Compromise' any member state was given the power to veto any proposal which it declared to be against its national interest.

The Commission's ill-fated 1965 package of proposals had included bringing forward the date of completion of the full customs union from 1970, as provided for in the Treaty of Rome, to 1 July 1967. The latter was the agreed date for the operation of common prices for cereals, eggs, pig and poultry meats and it seemed reasonable for intra-Community tariff barriers on industrial trade to be removed at the same time. In May 1966, almost a year after the French boycott, the Council, having returned to these matters, agreed to bring forward the full customs union by eighteen months to 1 July 1968, instead of the two and a half years proposed. Wider budgetary powers for the European Parliament, having caused so much trouble, were tactfully forgotten. The interim financing of the CAP to cover the remaining two and a half years of transition (1 July 1967 to 31 December 1969) was also settled. From 1967 FEOGA was, for the first time, to finance all CAP expenditures. FEOGA receipts were to be 90 per cent of all agricultural import levies and duties (10 per cent being considered to be national collection costs), any deficit being made up by national budgetary contributions according to a new fixed key (see Table Appendix 3.1.1).

Guidance Section expenditure had originally been set at one-third of the level of guarantee expenditure, with a ceiling of 100 million Units of Account (UA) (see Chapter 4) to apply in 1967. This ceiling was a recognition of the fact that Guarantee expenditures would rise rapidly as the price policy embraced more products, and there seemed no reason why Guidance expenditure should rise in proportion. By 1966 the expenditure ceiling looked rather low, and it was raised to 285 million UA for 1967 onwards. In practice this made the Guidance Section much more effective, because when it was limited to one-third of Guarantee expenditure the funds available were unknown until the latter's accounts were completed. Allocations were thus in arrears, and by the time submissions had been passed through national ministries and approved by FEOGA, something like two years had passed. Knowing how much was available in advance at least expedited decisions. Revenues for the Guidance Section were obtained by national contributions made on exactly the same bases as those for the Guarantee Section.

A DECADE OF ACHIEVEMENT

In 1967 the CAP was approaching completion. Its principles and policy instruments had been thrashed out in many hours of often painful negotiation. Opposing views and interests had somehow been reconciled in a spirit of determined compromise. The first products to come under the CAP reached the single market stage of common prices during the year. The details of policies affecting some major products were still being negotiated but it was clear that agreements would be reached.

The sense of progress in the Community was underlined by a second application for membership by the UK on 10 May 1967. Ireland, Denmark and Norway also applied (these enlargement matters are discussed later). On 1 July 1967 a Merger Treaty took effect, combining the EEC, and the ECSC and the European Atomic Energy Commission (EAEC). It had long been intended to merge the three Communities but agreement had been difficult; its achievement was another sign of the increasing pace of unification.

Whilst the CAP was a tribute to the determination of the Six to work together it was already clear that it was no panacea for all the ills of agriculture. Indeed, its emphasis on a policy of high prices designed to give farmers a 'fair' standard of living was treating the symptoms of the disease rather than attempting a cure, which would surely have paid more attention to the main cause of low incomes: too many farmers. A full critique of the CAP is reserved for later chapters. At this stage an appropriate summary of the situation is provided by a speech of the Agriculture Commissioner, Dr Sicco Mansholt, to the Council of Ministers of Agriculture on 17 October 1967. He explained that average incomes in agriculture remained low, and that raising them through further price rises would generate large surpluses for many products. Thus the CAP, although only approaching completion, was already nearing the limits of its potential. It required major changes aimed particularly at a reduction in the number of producers. The ministers were not pleased to be told that their hard-won policy needed fundamental alteration, but agreed that the Commission should prepare a report for their consideration.

The second decade of the EEC, 1968–77

This section covers the period when the CAP passed from a difficult childhood to become an even more difficult and controversial teenager. The early part of the decade saw the completion of the full customs union including common agricultural prices, though these were very soon lost. High support prices for agricultural products and the fruits of technological advances resulted in expanding surpluses, especially in the dairy sector; increasing surplus disposal costs consequently became a matter of growing concern and criticism. The Commission proposed to reduce, if not ultimately remove, the need for price support through an ambitious modernization programme, but action in this area was in practice modest. Finally, this section deals with the enlargement of the EEC and the issues involved in the negotiations, and, in the case of the UK, the renegotiation of the terms of membership.

THE COMPLETION OF THE PRICE POLICY

The Treaty of Rome had set 1 January 1970 as the date by which policies and prices were to be harmonized, but as noted in the previous part of this chapter, it was agreed in May 1966 to complete the process by 1 July 1968. Common prices and policies for most agricultural products had been agreed, with the notable exceptions of milk, beef and veal for which only provisional agreements had been reached.

In the early 1960s the Community was already self-sufficient in milk and dairy products, but subsequently, whilst supplies increased, consumption slowly declined. Problems of surplus production were already evident when provisional agreements on price levels had been reached in 1966, and in the spring of 1968 final arrangements had to be agreed before the 1 July deadline. With surpluses in mind, the Commission proposed a lower milk target price than had been provisionally settled in 1966. In fact it repeated its 1966 price proposals which had been overruled by the Council of Ministers. As before, the Council set higher prices, mindful of the overwhelming importance of milk to the majority of small farmers for whom the CAP existed. After protracted negotiations the details were agreed towards the end of May 1968, although translating them into regulations delayed implementation until 29 July. As cattle produce milk, beef and veal simultaneously the prices of the latter products had to be agreed at the same time; this was relatively easy, for there was no beef surplus at that time.

On 1 July 1968 the full customs union for all industrial products and most agricultural products came into force. The agricultural exceptions were wine, tobacco, fish, potatoes, sheepmeat and wool. Only the first three of these were to be governed by special policies introduced during the decade. The tobacco policy was introduced in February 1970. It provided intervention arrangements with a common system of marketing, and aimed to harmonize excise duties by 1980. Wine proved to be one of the most difficult products on which to agree. Proposals and counter-proposals were debated for seven years before agreement was reached in April 1970. This set customs duties and variable levies on imports and provided intervention arrangements similar to those for other products. In addition, regulations were much concerned with quality and included items such as the supervision of plantings. Regulations for fish were agreed in October 1970, to be effective from February 1971 (no more need be said about fish since the production conditions and historical developments peculiar to agriculture do not apply).

MONETARY INSTABILITY

This subject is discussed fully in Chapter 4, but to preserve the chronological perspective of the present chapter it must be introduced here. Common prices were denominated in terms of the Unit of Account (UA) and each national currency bore a fixed relationship (exchange rate) to it. In international trade fixed exchange rates were also normal, so that, for example, trade between Germany and the

USA occurred with marks and dollars exchanging at known constant rates. In 1969 the demand for Germany's exports was so strong that the demand for marks caused the exchange rate between marks and other currencies to be changed. Increases in the value of a currency such as occurred in this case to the mark are termed revaluations. Consider the consequences of this revaluation in Germany. The higher value of the mark meant that there were fewer marks to each unit of other currency than before. So imports into Germany had become cheaper and exports more expensive. These changes were really the result of German industries becoming relatively more competitive than those of other countries; after the revaluation, the competitive balance was restored by the lower prices of imports and the higher prices of exports. The higher value of the mark meant that there were fewer marks per UA than before. But common agricultural prices were defined in UA, so the prices of agricultural products paid in marks to German farmers needed to be reduced to preserve the common UA price. Such price reductions were not acceptable to German politicians, and it was decided to phase them in gradually over three years. Doubtless it was expected that price rises in terms of UAs would in the meantime remove the need actually to reduce prices in marks. Whether or not such hopes were entertained, the immediate effect was that German farmers were receiving higher prices than the common price level, their prices being calculated at the old mark/UA rate of exchange, which being thus retained was called a 'green' rate to distinguish it from the new market rate. With free trade within the EEC the higher German prices would obviously have drawn agricultural produce into Germany from all other members. Chaos was prevented by introducing monetary compensatory amounts (MCAs) to tax Germany's agricultural imports and subsidize her exports and so preserve the artificially high German prices.

Although the discussion above is in terms of the mark, the French franc was first to have its exchange rate altered. A franc devaluation of 11.11 per cent on 10 August 1969 should have resulted in higher prices for French farmers, but this would have exacerbated the existing rate of inflation. So the French government resisted the change, persuading the Council of Ministers to agree to a phased introduction of the new prices over two years for some products at least, others being realigned immediately. The German mark was 'floated' on 30 September, that is the market was allowed to determine the new rate of exchange; it was then fixed at a new level 8.5 per cent higher than before as from 26

October. Subsequently MCAs were introduced on agricultural trade between France, Germany and the other Community members. Common price levels had been short-lived; so far as agriculture was concerned the common market was now divided into three, each having its own set of prices. This was not to be the end of these problems; further exchange rate fluctuations and their consequence are detailed in Chapter 4.

SURPLUSES

In a free market surpluses cannot occur, because any excess of production over consumption at the prevailing market price will cause that price to fall, encouraging more consumption and less production. Thus markets move towards equilibrium where production and consumption are equated through price changes. Under the CAP prices are not allowed to fall below intervention levels because of the effect on farmers' incomes. When supplies exceed demand the intervention agencies purchase at the intervention price level and store the surplus.

When the CAP was devised the Six were net importers of nearly all major agricultural commodities. The intervention system was primarily intended to purchase *seasonal* surpluses following for example an unusually good harvest, and to sell stock later in the year when prices would otherwise rise. Thus prices would be stabilized to the benefit of both producers and consumers. The introduction of the CAP coincided with a period of marked scientific progress reflected in dramatically rising yields as shown in Table 3.2. Of course, in a society where people were already well fed and population growth was slight, total food consumption failed to increase in line with production. So under the rigid price system of the CAP, chronic rather than seasonal surpluses began to appear for several products. These had to be purchased and stored; their disposal became a serious problem.

Surpluses could not be sold on the Community market without depressing prices and defeating the object of the exercise; they could not be destroyed because destroying food is regarded as immoral and therefore politically unacceptable. Three outlets became important. First, some surpluses were sold to farmers at prices low enough to enable them to be fed to livestock. To remove the farmers' temptation to resell these feed bargains back into the higher priced normal markets, such surpluses were 'denatured'; wheat, for example, was

Table 3.2 Yields of some major products in EEC of Nine, 1955–80

	100 kg/ha		
	Cereals	Potatoes	Sugar beet
1955	23.7	172.7	332.5
1956	24.1	196.8	313.9
1957	23.9	188.0	338.0
1958	23.9	175.5	372.0
1959	25.6	178.8	297.2
1960	26.2	198.0	425.4
1961	25.1	191.0	365.3
1962	28.7	203.5	328.5
1963	28.4	218.7	372.4
1964	29.9	204.3	390.3
1965	30.4	207.5	375.3
1966	29.5	220.2	405.5
1967	34.0	243.2	425.6
1968	34.0	242.7	433.1
1969	34.2	235.5	419.0
1970	32.7	245.5	408.1
1971	37.3	259.8	447.6
1972	38.3	268.8	423.3
1973	39.6	268.1	441.0
1974	40.4	285.5	399.9
1975	36.9	243.1	405.7
1976	34.5	211.6	411.6
1977	40.0	271.1	450.3
1978	43.4	291.1	433.4
1979	42.6	290.0	445.4
1980	44.4	286.0	458.0

Sources: Statistical Office of the EC (1980, 1981)

contaminated with fish oil. Second, some surpluses were used to provide food aid for Third World countries. This is not the place for a full analysis of this topic but it must be said that non-emergency food aid is a mixed blessing – it induces dependence on the donor which may be used for political or commercial blackmail; it reduces food prices in the recipient countries thereby damaging the major and poorest sector of their economies, i.e. agriculture; the resources represented by the food aid might have been of more benefit if given in some other form, perhaps technical aid to improve the recipients' own

Table 3.3 FEOGA guarantee expenditures

Period	million Units of Account Expenditure	Period	million Units of Account Expenditure
1962-3	28.7	1972	2 094.0
1963-4	50.7	1973	3 174.2
1964-5	159.9	1974	3 277.9
1965-6	238.6	1975	4 821.5
1966-7	395.5	1976	5 365.0
1967-8	1039.1	1977	6 168.8
1968-9	1642.6	1978	9 278.6
2nd half of 1969	1688.9	1979	10 434.5
1970	2604.2	1980	11 314.9
1971	1514.0	1981	11 141.2
		1982 (provisional)	13 320.1
		1983 (forecast)	14 087.1

Sources: OECD (1974b); Statistical Office of the EC (1982); ECC (1982a)

agriculture. To return to outlets for surpluses, the third and major outlet is the world market, which entails selling commodities purchased at intervention prices at much lower world prices using export subsidies. Surplus disposal has proved to be very expensive and is the major source of expenditure from the Guarantee Section of FEOGA. Table 3.3 demonstrates the spectacular growth of support costs; unfortunately these costs, though large, are only the tip of the iceberg. A detailed examination of this area is undertaken below in Chapter 5; for the moment we concentrate on FEOGA which had to finance the escalating costs of intervention and subsidized exports.

FINANCING FEOGA

It will be remembered that during the first decade the issue of national contributions to FEOGA gave rise to frequent fierce struggles, including the French boycott of Community meetings for a period of six months. Under interim financing arrangements covering the period 1 July 1967 to 31 December 1969 (see Table Appendix 3.1.1), FEOGA was to finance all CAP guarantee expenditures, receiving all agricultural import levies plus national contributions as necessary according to a fixed key. These two and a half years were the last stage of the transitional period by the end of which a permanent system of financing was to be determined.

In a now traditional negotiating marathon, ending on 23 December 1969, rather close to the end-of-the-year deadline, the Council of Ministers agreed the definitive method of financing to be introduced for 1975 and the arrangements for the intervening years. It was designed to replace the old system under which national contributions to the Community were settled through often acrimonious negotiation by giving the Community its own independent revenue, or *resources propres* (own resources). The financial aspects of the agreement were remarkably similar to the Commission's earlier proposals which had led to the six-month French boycott from June 1965, the principal difference being the omission of extra budgetary powers for the European Parliament. Under the agreement levies on agricultural imports and customs duties on all goods (less 10 per cent regarded as collection costs) were to accrue to the Community. Expenditure in excess of this was to be met from national value added tax (VAT) receipts up to a maximum VAT rate of 1 per cent. Implicit in this agreement was the assumption that by 1975 the harmonization of member states' VAT systems would be achieved (in the event this proved not to be so and the VAT-based contributions were not implemented until 1979). It should be noted that the system of 'own resources' was to apply to the Community Budget as a whole, covering both agricultural expenditure through FEOGA and other non-agricultural elements of Community activities. FEOGA would, however, clearly be the major single item; during the 1970s it accounted for about three-quarters of the Community budget.

The transition from the old method of financing FEOGA to the new budgetary system was to be achieved gradually. In 1970 the whole of FEOGA expenditures were to be financed by national contributions according to a fixed key. From 1971 the Community received all agricultural import levies, and 50 per cent of customs duties, the latter increasing to 100 per cent in 1975. The balance of expenditure was to be met from national contributions according to yet another fixed key.

STRUCTURAL REFORM

Dr Mansholt's 1967 speech to the Council of Ministers warning them that the CAP required major changes has already been noted. Briefly, he said that the CAP had attempted to raise farm incomes by supporting prices but this had caused large surpluses to develop which were expensive to dispose of, without providing satisfactory incomes for the majority of farmers. The fundamental problem was one of too many farmers. It had been agreed that the Commission should produce proposals to reform the Community's agriculture. Accordingly, in October 1968 Dr Mansholt presented his analysis of the situation to the Commission. His report was adopted towards the end of December and submitted to the Council of Ministers.

The Mansholt Plan, as the *Memorandum sur la réforme de l'agriculture dans la Communauté Economique Européenne* (ECC 1968) was popularly known, rested fundamentally on the premise that the only practical way to increase farm incomes was for farms to become larger and more modern businesses. The corollary was that there must be fewer farms and farmers. As the *Memorandum* showed in a detailed statistical appendix, farms were generally very small, so that the average farmer could produce and sell very little and inevitably suffered a low income.

The major dual objective of the *Memorandum* was to create large efficient farms providing adequate incomes which would reduce the need for high market prices. Lower prices would in the long term reduce FEOGA support costs. A move towards lower prices which were more freely influenced by world markets would in itself improve the efficiency of the industry and make surpluses less likely as well as cheaper to dispose of.

To achieve these objectives the *Memorandum* said that it would be necessary to facilitate the removal of 5 million people from agriculture in the years 1970–80. To encourage this exodus farmers should be offered retirement pensions, or compensation plus retraining for other occupations. Financial assistance of various types would permit the remaining farms to be enlarged and modernized. Such farms would be more productive, and to prevent their additional output exacerbating surplus problems it was suggested that 5 million hectares should be taken out of agriculture, largely for re-afforestation; this would also benefit the Community by reducing its dependence on imported timber supplies. The Commission realized that to prevent rural depopulation and corresponding urban congestion regional policies would be required to bring jobs to rural areas. They estimated that (provided the Community maintained its current growth rate of about 3 per cent per year) there would be sufficient new jobs created to absorb the ex-farmers.

The reactions of farmer organizations to the Plan varied from coolly critical to very hostile. To many, the proposals appeared to involve social engineering on a scale unprecedented in free societies. Dr Mansholt was dubbed 'the peasant killer'. The fact that between 1958 and 1968 about 5 million people had already left agriculture, so that the Plan merely attempted to encourage a continuation of this trend, was ignored. Politicians – ever wary of the voting power of farmers and harried by the agricultural lobbies – found the Plan embarrassing, so much so that it was never formally discussed by the Council of Ministers.

Despite its unfortunate reception, the *Memorandum* was far from wasted. It shocked all sides of Community agriculture into a greater awareness of the problems and thus made somewhat milder Community structural policies easier to introduce later. One of its major elements, however, was to continue to be firmly resisted – the severing of the connection between prices and incomes; indeed the support of prices at high levels was to remain the main plank of policy.

In 1972 the seeds of reform sown by Dr Mansholt bore some fruit. Three directives were adopted which for the first time provided a Community approach towards structural problems. The *Modernisation of farms* (EEC 1972a) offered FEOGA grants of up to 25 per cent of modernization costs for farmers whose incomes were near or below the average non-agricultural income of their area. To qualify, farmers had to possess 'adequate professional ability', to agree to work to an approved six-year development plan and to keep proper accounts (the latter being virtually non-existent on most farms). Farmers participating in this scheme were to have first refusal of land released under the second directive. This, the *Cessation of Farming and the Reallocation of Agricultural Land for Structural Improvement* (EEC 1972b) offered farmers over the age of 55 either lump-sum payments or annuities to leave agriculture. Vacated land could be sold or leased to another farmer; alternatively member states could purchase it and use it for non-agricultural purposes, generally either leisure or afforestation. The leasing provision recognized the reluctance of small peasant farmers to sell their land even if they and their families left agriculture, for land is a uniquely secure asset. To ensure that old farmers could not easily change their minds and begin farming again, land leased to other farmers under this directive had to be for a minimum of twelve years. FEOGA would again finance up to 25 per cent of the costs of this directive, except that in areas of extremely small low-income farms –

in Ireland and Italy – FEOGA's rate of contribution could rise to 65 per cent.

The third directive was the *Provision of Socio-economic Guidance* (ECC 1972c). It was primarily intended to help farmers to improve their incomes through training to improve their farming skills or by expanding their businesses into non-agricultural activities, most commonly tourism. Additionally, farmers and workers were to be helped to assess and compare their prospects in agriculture with opportunities outside.

The thrust of these three directives is simultaneously to reduce the number of farmers and expand the average size of farm so that farm incomes will increase. Such a policy is reinforcing the 'natural' forces of economic development discussed in Chapter 1, forces which the main element of policy – price support – has clearly weakened. However, a further major exodus of population out of agriculture is not necessarily an unmixed blessing. Indeed in some areas, notably the remoter mountainous areas, the post-war exodus has been large enough to create other problems. In such areas agriculture was the major source of income so that the loss of farm folk reduced the sales of rural shops and garages and caused the closure of some schools: in short, the social and economic structure began to disintegrate whilst the costs of providing public services such as transport, education and medical facilities, all increased. Existing high-price policies were insufficient to raise farm incomes in such regions to reasonable levels. The three new directives were on balance likely to increase the rate of labour migration. Consequently, in 1975 a new directive *Mountain and Hill Farming and Farming in Certain Less-favoured Areas* (ECC 1975a) was introduced, aiming to stem the tide of depopulation. Less favoured areas are mountainous and/or remote, generally with harsh production conditions so that output and incomes are low. When the measure was introduced it was estimated to apply to about one-quarter of the Community's agricultural area and 20 per cent of its farms. To benefit, farmers in these regions have to promise to stay in farming for at least five years. They then receive annually a subsidy – a 'compensatory amount' – which varies according to the severity of their locality's natural handicaps.

The Less-favoured Areas directive is clearly dealing with problems which in some important aspects are different from the problems of agriculture in other 'normal' regions. Whilst, apart from this directive, the CAP is preoccupied with the 'normal' regions, the large numbers of people and areas of land involved should not be overlooked. Occasionally, these less favoured areas force themselves into public notice, a notable example being the sheepmeat battles of the late 1970s.

EEC ENLARGEMENT

The collapse of enlargement negotiations in 1963 was noted earlier. British politicians had favoured membership then for primarily political reasons. These remained the same – the desire to join a large group which collectively would be a world power to compensate for the UK's decline relative to the 'super powers'. Economic motives now began to reinforce the case for membership. In 1963 GNP per head in the UK was 10 per cent above the Community average. More rapid economic growth in the EEC rapidly reversed this position; indeed by 1973 when accession took place the UK's GNP per head was only 70 per cent of that of the Six (ECC 1975b, 15).

On 10 November 1966 the Prime Minister, Mr Harold Wilson, announced to the House of Commons plans to approach the EEC with a view to full membership. Accordingly the early months of 1967 saw exploratory discussions between the UK and each of the six current members. These were sufficiently encouraging for Mr Wilson to announce in the House of Commons on 2 May 1967 that the UK would apply for a second time to join the EEC. This she did on 11 May, followed by Ireland, Denmark and Norway.

The first enlargement negotiations had been particularly difficult because they came at a time when the Community's policies were still being formulated. Those policies were now settled and it was expected that negotiations this time would be easier. However, before they could begin General de Gaulle, in another press conference in November 1967, said that in his view UK membership would destroy the Community. In the following month five member states expressed themselves in favour of opening enlargement negotiations, but France objected and so the matter had to be dropped. The UK stated that its application remained 'on the table'. In 1969 General de Gaulle resigned, and his successor (President Pompidou) clearly held different views, for at the Hague Summit held in December of that year the leaders of the Six agreed to open negotiations with the four applicants.

Agriculture was the key area for the negotiators of each of the applicants. The CAP as it stood would benefit both Ireland and

Denmark (as will become clear in subsequent chapters). Because of the harsh climate and physical conditions Norway's agriculture was even more protected than that of the EEC. For the UK, the CAP seemed likely to present serious balance-of-payments problems, to be contrary to her traditional cheap food policy and to present serious difficulties for some Commonwealth countries which were substantially dependent upon the UK market for their exports of agricultural produce. This applied particularly to New Zealand for whom dairy products were the single largest export, 85 per cent going to the UK, and to a number of developing countries who, under the Commonwealth Sugar Agreement, sent most of their sugar to the UK. As members of EFTA, three applicants (i.e. excluding Ireland) had also to consider their obligations to this trading group. In practice there were no difficulties here, the non-applicant members of EFTA reaching a free trade agreement covering industrial products with the EEC.

By the time negotiations began in June 1970 the Labour government had been replaced by the Conservatives under Mr Edward Heath. The new administration was more strongly in favour of joining the EEC than its predecessor had been, and negotiations proceeded rapidly. They were successfully completed in June 1971, the date of accession begin set for 1 January 1973. The terms of accession were published in July 1971 in a White Paper (HM Government 1971). This White Paper also stated the political and economic case for accession and discussed the costs and problems likely to be involved. The major cost was expected to be caused by the CAP, and was expected to be large (although accurate forecasts were not possible). The economic benefits were altogether more nebulous in conception and the White Paper's conclusion is largely a statement of faith:

> the government are confident that membership of the enlarged Community will lead to much improved efficiency and productivity in British industry, with a higher rate of investment and a faster growth of real wages .... These improvements in efficiency and competitive power should enable the United Kingdom to meet the balance of payments costs of entry over the next decade as they gradually build up. (paras 56, 57)

Under the terms of accession the UK was to adopt the CAP in its entirety. The CAP *system* was to be adopted immediately upon accession, but recognizing that CAP prices were considerably higher than food prices in the UK, the necessary price increases were to be introduced gradually in a series of approximately equal annual steps; the final step to full CAP prices was to be on 1 January 1978. This transitional period was applied to other areas of the economy also, such as the adoption of the Community's industrial imports tariffs.

Arrangements to cater for New Zealand's interests were difficult to achieve. Since the late nineteenth century food produced cheaply and efficiently in New Zealand had reached, indeed been designed for, the British market. British consumers had benefited from these cheap food imports. New Zealand had ready access to a large and stable market; especially for her dairy products and lamb, she was to a considerable extent dependent on the British market. There was no Community policy for sheepmeat, and the imposition of a 20 per cent tariff on New Zealand lamb was expected to have little effect on its export to Britain. Dairy products were far more of a problem; indeed, the Community had had a surplus of butter since its inception, and doubtless hoped to dispose of it on the British market. The UK refused to agree to this since it would have amounted to the virtual destruction of New Zealand's dairy industry. Eventually, it was agreed that New Zealand would have continued but reduced access to the UK market. Her butter exports to the UK were to be reduced by 4 per cent per year during the transitional period, so that in 1977 she would still be able to send 80 per cent of previous levels; cheese was to be reduced much more, to 20 per cent of previous levels. For these sales New Zealand was to be guaranteed prices equivalent to at least the average of the years 1969–72. In the third year after accession the position of New Zealand butter was to be examined with the objective of providing continued access after 1977.

Under the Commonwealth Sugar Agreement the UK imported cane sugar from many countries, mostly developing countries to some of whom sugar exports were very important. It was agreed that the UK should honour existing contractual arrangements, due to expire in 1974. The Community undertook to negotiate special trade agreements to safeguard the interests of developing country Commonwealth sugar producers after that date.

Throughout the enlargement negotiations it was recognized that adoption of the CAP would impose heavy balance-of-payments costs on the UK. There were two elements to this cost: firstly the UK would have to pay high CAP prices for food imports instead of the low world prices previously enjoyed, secondly the UK would have to make some contribution to the Community budget – the bulk of whose expenditure was on the CAP. These items are discussed in more detail in Chapter 6; for the moment we concentrate on the UK's contribution to the budget. The UK proposed an initial contribution of 3 per cent rising to 15 per cent by the end of the transition period. The Commission proposed a UK contribution of either 21.5 per cent or a progressive increase from 10–15 per cent initially to 20–25 per cent ultimately. A compromise set of figures was accepted, rising from 8.6 per cent in 1973 to 18.92 per cent in 1977. Subsequently, the UK might have been expected to be subject to the existing Community budget system, however for 1978 it was agreed that her contribution should not rise above the 1977 level by more than two-fifths of the difference between the 1977 contribution and the Commission's estimate of what the 1978 contribution would have been under the full system. A similar calculation applied to 1979, but from then on the UK was to be subject to the existing budgetary arrangements. In short, the UK accepted the EEC's method of financing the budget as it stood, following a transitional period and some cushioning for the next two years. Contributions from 1980 onwards were impossible to calculate as the 1971 White Paper acknowledges; however, it goes on to state:

it is for this reason that the Community declared to us during the course of the negotiations that if unacceptable situations should arise 'the very survival of the Community would demand that the institutions find equitable solutions'. (para. 96)

Negotiations were successfully completed for all the four applicant countries, but Norway did not join, her people rejecting membership in a national referendum. However, Norway was able to enjoy free industrial trade with the Community under the agreement made with the non-applicant members of EFTA.

BRITISH RENEGOTIATION

The UK's application to join the EEC had been made with a Labour government in power; the terms of accession had been agreed by the following Conservative government, but the Labour Opposition had described them as unacceptable. Their main objections were the effects of the CAP on food prices and the balance of payments. In February 1974 Labour returned to power and demanded the renegotiation of the terms of membership, promising to place any new settlement before the nation either in a referendum or general election.

The British position was set out in a White Paper (HM Government 1974). The main points were as noted above, that the agreed method of financing the budget was expected to become an unfair burden on the balance of payments and that other consequences of the adoption of the CAP were also unsatisfactory. A further worry was that the objective of Economic and Monetary Union (EMU) by 1980 (adopted at the Hague Summit of 1969 and discussed in Chapter 4) was too ambitious. There were, of course, a number of other less important matters raised. Gradually, these issues were settled during the following year, the last problem being that of the UK budgetary contribution. This was agreed at the Dublin Summit of March 1975 and on 5 July the first-ever British referendum took place. The electorate was asked: 'Do you think the UK should stay in the European Community (The Common Market)?'; 17 millions voted 'Yes' and 8 millions 'No'.

What was achieved by this renegotiation? In the first place there was a great deal of irritation in the remainder of the EEC that 'perfidious Albion' should want to change the terms after only one year of membership. The new terms were not really different in any significant way from their 'unacceptable' predecessors. EMU had become unfashionable – which the British politicians should have known – a pipe dream rather than a realistic objective. The Community promised a full-scale reappraisal of the CAP which was certainly not a commitment to change it in any way. Finally, there was the Dublin Summit agreement to modify the UK budgetary contribution: this is of some importance and merits close attention.

Before the 'own resources' financial system had been agreed the national contributions to the Community had been approximately in proportion to GNP. Under the new system 90 per cent of customs duties and agricultural levies (10 per cent being collection cost), plus a contribution of up to a maximum of a 1 per cent VAT rate was paid to the Community. The VAT-based contribution was clearly proportional to GNP, but the other contributions depended upon imports. So a country which was a major importer of food or raw materials could contribute a much larger share than under a GNP-based system. At the Dublin Summit it had been admitted that the new system might result in a country paying an unduly large contribution and that a refund should be paid if this happened. The agreement defined an unduly large contribution as being more than 110 per cent of a country's share of Community GNP. Other conditions would have to be satisfied before a country could receive a refund. Its GNP per head would have to be less than 85 per cent of the Community average, its real rate of growth less than 120 per cent of the Community average and its contributions would have to exceed its receipts. Refunds were to be on a sliding scale and subject to a ceiling of 250 million UAs, or to 3 per cent of the budget if this rose above 8000 million UAs.

As the UK satisfied all the conditions for a refund should her contributions exceed 110 per cent of her share of GNP, these terms were accepted. However, it is important to note that the contributions referred to are *gross*. Like any other budget, the purpose of the EEC budget is to finance expenditure. Since most of this is on the CAP relatively little is received by the UK (see Chapter 6), so that even if the UK *gross* budgetary contribution was proportional to her share of Community GNP she would still pay out large sums in *net* terms and this would still be a major burden on the balance of payments. These matters are returned to in detail in Chapter 6, but they are mentioned here because of their importance in the context of renegotiations. There are two possible explanations for the UK's acceptance of a settlement which was so unfavourable to her: either the British negotiators or politicians involved were incompetent (perhaps gross incompetence is the appropriate expression) or the politicians, having failed to achieve much better terms in their renegotiation, were reluctant to admit their failure. On 18 March 1975 the Prime Minister stated: 'I believe that our renegotiation objectives have been substantially though not completely achieved' (HM Government 1975, 8). The government commented on the budget issue as follows: 'Under the previous terms, Britain's contribution to the Common Market budget imposed too heavy a burden on us. The new terms ensure that Britain will pay a fairer share' (ibid., 9). The use of the word *fairer* rather than fair suggests that the government was not entirely happy with the settlement.

Bibliography

In addition to the sources referred to specifically in the text of this chapter, the following have been extensively used:

Butterwick, M. and Rolfe, E. N. (1971) *Agricultural Marketing and the EEC*, London, Hutchinson.

de la Mahotiere, S. (1961) *The Common Market*, London, Hodder & Stoughton.

Swann, D. (1978) *The Economics of the Common Market*, 4th edn, Harmondsworth, Penguin.

Tracy, M. (1964) *Agriculture in Western Europe*, London, Jonathan Cape.

Appendix 3.1 Institutional and financial arrangements of the Community

Council of Ministers. This is the highest decision-making body in the Community. Its composition varies with the subject area; for agricultural matters it comprises the agriculture ministers of each country. In its most senior form the Council consists of the foreign ministers, in which form it has to date been responsible for major financial decisions such as budgetary contributions.

Council decisions may be taken by weighted voting but generally unanimity is sought; the power of veto is accepted under the Luxembourg Compromise. In the exceptional cases where a vote is taken and no power of veto is exercised, a majority means at least forty-five votes from six countries, the voting weights are:

10 Germany, France, Italy, UK;
 5 Netherlands, Belgium, Greece;
 3 Denmark, Ireland;
 2 Luxembourg.

Commission. A body of fourteen Commissioners who each has charge of one or more Directorates General. The latter constitute a Community-level civil service. Although the Commission cannot make policy decisions it is the major source of policy initiatives; it can take 'non-controversial' decisions in areas such as regulations to implement agreed policy decisions. The Agricultural Directorate (DG VI) is the most prestigious of the Directorates General because of the exceptional importance of the CAP.

European Parliament. Originally an assembly appointed by member governments, it has been directly elected since 1979; elections are to be held every five years.

Its main power is to dismiss the Commission by carrying a vote of censure by a two-thirds majority. It also has to examine and agree the Community budget. The Parliament's role is consultative rather than decision-making; all Commission proposals have to be passed to it for an opinion before being placed before the Council.

Economic and Social Committee. An appointed body representing a wide spectrum of interests: producers, processors, distributors, consumers and trade unionists. Commission proposals are examined before being passed to the Council; originally entirely consultative, the Committee now has the right to make policy proposals.

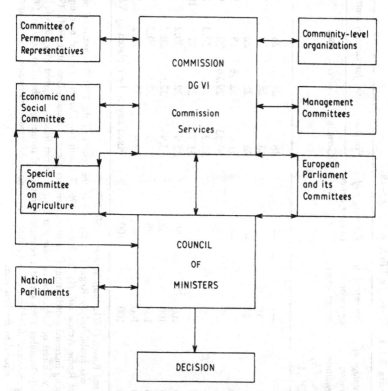

Figure Appendix 3.1.1 Policy decision-making in the Community. The Commission formulates proposals which are discussed by all affected or interested parties. Their opinions are passed to the Commission and/or Council and may result in any eventual decision being significantly different from the original proposal.

Table Appendix 3.1.1 Financing FEOGA 1962/3–1975

	Percentage of guarantee expenditure financed by FEOGA	Percentage of agricultural import levies	Percentage of customs duties	Fixed key scales for national contributions					
				Germany	France	Italy	Netherlands	Belgium	Luxembourg
1962/3	17⅔	—	—	28	28	28	7.9	7.9	0.2
1963/4	33⅓	10	—	28	28	28	7.9	7.9	0.2
1964/5	50	20	—	28	28	28	7.9	7.9	0.2
1965/6	60	—	—	31.67	32.58	18	9.58	7.95	0.22
1966/7	70	—	—	30.83	29.26	22	9.74	7.95	0.22
1967/9	100	90	—	31.2	32	20.3	8.2	8.1	0.2
1970	100	—	—	31.7	28	21.5	10.35	8.25	0.2
1971	100	100	50	32.9	32.6	20.2	7.3	6.8	0.2
1972	100	100	62.5	32.9	32.6	20.2	7.3	6.8	0.2
1973	100	100	75	32.9	32.6	20.2	7.3	6.8	0.2
1974	100	100	87.5	32.9	32.6	20.2	7.3	6.8	0.2
1975	100	100	100	Fixed key to be replaced by VAT-based contributions					

Sources: Marsh and Ritson (1971, 168); Strasser (1980, 377).

Notes: FEOGA was established by Regulation 25, one of the results of the 1961/2 negotiating marathon. Initial fixed key according to Treaty of Rome Article 200 (1). 1965/6 and 1966/7 Italian contributions reduced to compensate for higher priced feeding stuffs necessitating increased contributions from other members (Council decision December 1964). 1967–9 an eighteen-month period to align FEOGA with rest of budget on calendar year basis – interim financing agreed May 1966 following 'vacant chair' crisis. The Hague summit of December 1969 agreed a permanent method of financing to be introduced by 1975 – the 'own resources' system, 1970 financing by interim fixed key. 1971–4 actual contributions restricted to maximum variation upwards of 1 per cent and downwards of 1.5 per cent compared to previous year.

Court of Justice. Consists of ten judges acceptable to all member governments. Interprets and administers Community Law, ensuring its observance in all member states.

Committee of Permanent Representatives. Made up of Special Ambassadors to the Community, this Committee is consulted on major issues by the Commission.

Special Committee on Agriculture. A body of experts which examines issues on behalf of the Council before the latter body deals with them.

Management Committees. Each commodity has its own committee composed of government officials. Their role is to help the Commission to devise regulations implementing Council decisions in such a way as to ensure appropriate application under diverse national circumstances.

Appendix 3.2 Methods of support used by the CAP

PRICE SUPPORT

There are four ways in which the CAP raises farm prices above their free market levels. This section is a brief factual record; many of the terms used are explained in a glossary at the end of the appendix.

Intervention support

Soft wheat, barley, maize. Target prices are fixed annually; they relate to the area of greatest deficit, Duisburg in the Ruhr Valley. Target prices in other areas are derived by subtraction of transport costs. Threshold prices, which are the lowest prices at which imports may occur, are calculated so that when grain landed at Rotterdam is transported to Duisburg the target price will be slightly exceeded. If imports are offered at prices lower than the threshold levels the difference is made up by a variable levy; these are calculated every twenty-four hours. The system is designed to prevent imports undermining target prices.

If there is an internal surplus prices are prevented from falling greatly by intervention purchasing of surpluses. Intervention prices are 12–20 per cent below target prices. Both intervention and threshold prices are stepped seasonally, reflecting the trend of storage costs.

Intervention surpluses may be sold on the world market through the use of export subsidies.

Wheat of bread-making quality has a special reference price at which intervention can take place if the Commission so wishes. This higher price is a quality premium. Cereals have become subject to a kind of co-responsibility levy in 1983 as explained in Appendix 8.1.

Sugar. Prices are supported through target, intervention and threshold prices, variable levies and export subsidies, in much the same way as for the cereals discussed above. In addition output is subject to a quota and levy system so that producers have to finance the disposals of surpluses on the co-responsibility principle (this system was agreed in 1981, so FEOGA expenditures on sugar in future should be much less than in the past).

The Community has an 'A' quota of sugar, approximately equivalent to home consumption, and a 'B' quota. When the world price is lower than the Community price the cost of exporting the surplus is borne by a levy of 2 per cent on both 'A' and 'B' quota sugar, an additional levy on 'B' quota sugar may raise the total levy to 30 per cent. If costs exceed these levies, a supplementary levy of up to 7½ per cent may be ear-marked from the following season's 'B' quota. Output beyond the two quotas is entirely unsupported and must be sold for what it will fetch on the world market.

Under the Lomé Convention between the Community and certain African, Caribbean and Pacific developing countries the Community is committed to importing about 1.3 million tonnes of cane sugar. In case of surpluses the cost of disposing of this quantity of sugar is to be borne by the development policy budget and not by FEOGA.

Milk. The target price for milk is maintained by intervention for butter and skim milk (and cheese in Italy, since little butter is made there). All milk product prices are protected from imports by threshold prices, which are related by processing costs to the milk target price. Export subsidies for butter and skim milk powder have proved so expensive that a co-responsibility levy was introduced in 1977, for the 1982/83 year this was 2 per cent. Further price reductions as a result of exceeding a pre-set threshold output level in 1982 are detailed in Appendix 8.1.

Each year the Community gives 200,000 tonnes of skim milk powder to the World Food Programme.

Beef and veal.   A guide price is set, and the intervention price is 90 per cent of this. Variable import levies and export subsidies also apply. As an alternative to intervention, used in the UK only, a variable premium scheme operates: if the average market price falls below the target price level – 85 per cent of guide price – producers are paid a premium to make up the difference (this is very similar to the previously existing UK deficiency payments scheme).

Live cattle imports are subject to a duty of 16 per cent and carcase beef imports to a duty of 20 to 26 per cent depending on type. Variable import levies are fixed weekly: they are calculated as the difference between the guide price and the duty-paid import price, but the proportion of this levy to be paid depends on the state of the Community market. This is assessed in terms of the reference price – a weighted average market price for the Community. When the reference price is 98–100 per cent of the guide price the full levy is payable, when the reference price is above or below the guide price the proportion of the levy payable is decreased or increased.

Pigmeat.   For pigs the desired price is called a basic price. If the reference price (average market price) falls to between 85 and 92 per cent of the basic price, intervention buying takes place; the timing and extent of intervention is a matter for the discretion of the Commission in consultation with the Management Committee for pigs.

Imports are controlled by a system of 'sluice-gate' prices and levies. The sluice-gate price, fixed every quarter, is the estimated cost of production in third countries. If imports are offered below the sluice-gate price they are raised to this level by a supplementary levy. In addition a basic levy is charged. This is designed to allow for the difference between grain prices in the EEC and the world market plus 7 per cent of the previous year's sluice-gate prices as a margin of preference. Export subsidies may be granted to permit the disposal of surpluses.

Fruit and vegetables (cauliflowers, tomatoes, dessert grapes, peaches, apples, pears and citrus fruits).   Basic prices are fixed annually. Buying-in prices are set between 40 and 70 per cent of the basic price depending on the commodity. If a product's market price falls below its buying-in price for three consecutive days, a state of serious crisis may be declared by the Commission; member states must then intervene by purchasing produce until the buying-in price is exceeded for three consecutive days.

Producer organizations may fix withdrawal prices below which their members will not offer produce for sale; member states can specify maxima for these prices. If producer organizations withhold produce from the market these surpluses, and those of the official intervention agencies, must be disposed of in such a way that they will not re-enter normal markets; for example they may be fed to animals, processed or given to welfare organizations. Producer organizations are entitled to some compensation from Community funds for their withdrawal of produce from the market.

Imports are controlled by the imposition of countervailing charges. These are the difference between the offered import prices and reference prices, where the latter are based on costs of production and marketing. In addition customs duties of 10–21 per cent for vegetables and 7–25 per cent for fruit are applied. Surpluses may be exported with the aid of subsidies.

Wine. Prices are maintained by customs duties, variable import levies and market intervention.

Import controls

Eggs and poultrymeat. Prices are supported entirely through trade measures. Sluice-gate prices are fixed quarterly as estimates of production costs in third countries. A basic levy is applied, being based on the difference between Community and third-country production costs due to the former's high cereal prices, plus 7 per cent of the previous year's sluice-gate prices. If imports are offered at prices below the sluice-gate level the difference is charged as a supplementary levy.

The Commission may grant export subsidies to enable exporters to sell these products on world markets.

Miscellaneous. A wide variety of horticultural products and rice are similarly supported through import restrictions.

Variable price subsidies

These apply to a number of relatively minor products which cannot have their prices raised through import restrictions because customs duties on them have been agreed in GATT at nil or low levels. Guide and intervention prices are fixed for these products; deficiency payments are made to bridge the gap between the intervention and world market price. The products involved include tobacco, durum wheat, olive oil, oilseeds and, since 1980, sheepmeat.

For sheepmeat support is related to a reference price which is the Community's desired market price. If the average market price for the year is below the reference price the deficiency is made up as a headage payment on each breeding ewe at the end of the year. In France, if the price falls significantly below the reference level – to the basic price level – the market may be supported by intervention. A different system operates in the UK, where the reference price is seasonally stepped as weekly guide prices. If the average market price falls below the guide price, the sellers of fat lamb in that week are paid the difference as a 'variable slaughter premium'. These variable slaughter premia are subtracted when the annual ewe headage payment is calculated. Exporters of lamb to other EEC countries have to repay the variable premium; this is termed the clawback, and is necessary to protect lamb prices in the other EEC markets.

Flat rate subsidies

These are subsidies paid at a constant rate per hectare or unit of output. The products covered are of relatively slight importance and include cottonseed, flax, hemp, hops, seed, dried fodder and silkworms.

STRUCTURAL SUPPORT

Structural policy embraces a wide diversity of measures intended to improve the structure of individual farms and the agricultural production and marketing infrastructure of whole regions. In theory, structural measures were to be part of Community programmes and to be co-ordinated with general economic policy and regional development policy. The first measure, Regulation No. 17/64/EEC of 1964, granted aid from the Guidance Section of FEOGA for the financing of individual projects. Despite the expectation that these *ad hoc* projects would rapidly give way to Community programmes this did not happen for eight years. Then in 1972 three interrelated directives were adopted:

Modernisation of Farms (EEC 1972a). Member states were permitted to introduce selective schemes for modernization; this was intended to help farmers with low incomes compared to their region's non-agricultural incomes. Aid was restricted to full-time farmers who would work to an approved six-year development plan, and keep farm accounts. FEOGA could give grants of up to 25 per cent of modernization costs. Farmers participating in this scheme were to have the first option on land released under the second directive.

Producer groups were also to be encouraged. These are small groups of farmers who work co-operatively, sharing some equipment and co-ordinating their activities to improve efficiency. Aid could be granted for the launching of new groups or towards the management costs of existing groups.

Cessation of Farming and the Reallocation of Agricultural Land for Structural Improvement (EEC 1972b).   This directive provided for lump-sum or annuity payments to be made to farmers aged between 55 and 65 years as an incentive to accelerate their departure from agriculture. Their land could be leased or sold to other farmers (see previous directive) or withdrawn from agriculture.

Provision of Socio-economic Guidance (ECC 1972c).   This directive was to help the other two to work, firstly by encouraging farmers to acquire occupational training to enable them to modernize more effectively; secondly by providing advice to farmers who were considering ceasing farming so that their decisions would be taken in the light of all available information.

The effectiveness of these three directives was expected to be slight in remote or mountainous regions, so the Community adopted in 1975 a further directive: *Mountain and Hill Farming and Farming in Certain Less-favoured Areas* (ECC 1975a). This was intended to compensate farmers for the permanent natural handicaps of these areas and so to encourage them to continue in farming, so preserving a minimum population and ensuring the conservation of these rural environments.

In 1977 Regulation No. 355/77/EEC was introduced to improve the conditions under which agricultural products are processed and marketed. FEOGA could finance up to 25 per cent (30 per cent in less favoured areas) of investment costs, with member states contributing at least 5 per cent; the investors themselves had to find at least 50 per cent.

THE DEVELOPMENT OF THE CAP 57

Producer groups. It has long been believed that the small outputs of most farmers give them a very weak bargaining position in the market place. Producer groups which are small enough to ensure good market discipline but large enough to exploit economies of size in marketing have been particularly favoured by the Commission. In 1970 it was estimated that such groups accounted for about 14 per cent of Community output, and the Commission proposed an increase to over 60 per cent during the decade (ECC 1970, pt VI). Accordingly a variety of measures granting launching aid, investment aid and training for managers and staff have been introduced. The first measures were introduced for fruit and vegetables in 1966 and it is in this sector that they are most appropriate. This is because horticultural products are either not subject to price support under the CAP or the degree of support is less than for other commodities, yet output is very seasonal and perishable, yields and prices often fluctuating violently in rather localized markets.

Mediterranean policy. The farm structure of the Mediterranean areas of the Community is particularly unfavourable, and so is the infrastructure. To bring about some improvement in these, the poorest agricultural areas of the Community, a variety of extra measures has been introduced. Regulation No. 355/77 was amended in several respects in 1978 to give more generous FEOGA support to producer groups and to other processing and marketing projects in these areas. Measures include irrigation in the Mezzogiorno and in Corsica. Regulation No. 1760/78 EEC introduced common measures to improve *public amenities* in 'certain rural areas'. Aid projects are concerned with the provision of clean water, electricity and improved roads. It is believed that such amenities are essential to further agricultural development.

A 'New' structural policy was adopted by the Council in April 1981 (ECC 1981a). Basically this was a series of amendments to the 1972 Modernisation of farms and Social-economic Guidance directives to make them apply more generously in terms of FEOGA support to the less-favoured areas of the Mediterranean regions and the West of Ireland. The only new aspect of the policy is a swing in emphasis away from the 'normal' regions, where implementation of the directives has tended to expand output and thus exacerbate surpluses, and towards the less-favoured areas.

GLOSSARY

Based on the Commission's glossary in *The Agricultural Policy of the European Community*, 3rd edn, 1981.

Basic price: applies to pigmeat, fruit and vegetables. When market prices fall below the basic price the market may be supported by buying in surplus output.

Co-responsibility: the principle that farmers must share in the financial responsibility for dealing with surplus production.

Customs duties: are at a fixed *ad valorem* rate on industrial products and also on some agricultural products imported from outside the EEC, e.g. 16 per cent on live cattle, 20 per cent on beef and veal. Various rates apply on fruits and vegetables. Duties can be reduced or suspended by the Council of Ministers.

Export refunds (or restitutions): subsidies paid to enable Community traders to export at world prices when these are significantly lower than EEC prices.

Green currencies: special ('reference' or 'representative' or 'green') exchange rates used for the purposes of the CAP

Guide price: a price fixed annually for beef cattle or sheep at a level considered desirable for producers under normal market conditions. It is used as a basis for determining support buying prices and variable levies.

Intervention price: the price at which the Community undertakes to support the market by purchasing and storing produce.

Levy: a variable charge on imports or exports. On imports from outside the Community, it brings import prices up to the threshold price (e.g. for cereals) or is calculated on the basis of a formula (e.g. pigs, eggs and poultry). When world prices are higher than Community prices it may be applied to exports.

MCA (Monetary Compensatory Amounts): levies or subsidies designed to compensate for currency fluctuations in EEC farm trade.

Reference price: the minimum import price for fruit and vegetables. Produce entering the EEC from non-member countries at below the reference price may be charged a countervailing duty.

For beef, veal and pigmeat the reference price is the official average weekly market price, based on weighted averages of national figures. For sheep the reference price fixes the overall level of support given to producers.

Sluice-gate price: a form of minimum import price applied to pigmeat, eggs and poultry. It is intended to represent the cost of production in non-member countries. A levy is paid on imports above this price and a supplementary levy on imports coming into the Community below the sluice-gate price.

Target price: a prescribed price at which Community policy is aiming. It is supported by import levies, export subsidies and intervention measures.

Threshold price: the lowest price at which imports can cross the Community's frontier without undermining the target price. When the lowest offer price of imports is below the threshold price, a levy, representing the difference, is chargeable.

Withdrawal price: the price at which producer groups can withdraw certain fruit and vegetables from the market.

4 Monetary problems

In this chapter we consider the units in which agricultural prices are denominated and the artificial exchange rates employed in translating them into national currencies. This is followed by an examination of the effects of the 'green currencies' system on common prices and competition. Finally the possible solution to these problems – 'economic and monetary union' – is analysed both with respect to agriculture and (more briefly) to the broader national economic issues involved.

Units of Account

When the Community introduced common policies it adopted a unit of account (UA) in which to denominate its financial transactions. It could have chosen to use an existing national currency, but preferred to emphasize its supranational nature by defining a special new currency. Accordingly a UA was introduced, defined in terms of gold and conveniently equivalent in value to the US dollar which at that time was convertible into gold. Under the post-war system of currency exchange rates then operating, national currencies exchanged for one another at fixed rates. So when the common prices stage of the CAP was reached and the Community set a target price for (say) wheat, this would be in terms of UAs; when this price was translated into national currencies all the target prices for wheat would be the same in real terms in each country. Thus the CAP would achieve common prices within a common market despite the existence of different national currencies, but Community-level decisions would be in terms of its own supranational currency.

Green currencies

The 1969 revaluation of the German mark and devaluation of the French franc were discussed in the previous chapter (p. 34). Since

agricultural prices were set in terms of UAs, the new higher value
mark should have resulted in lower German farm prices in marks;
similarly, the lower value franc should have given French farmers a
price increase in terms of francs. In neither case did the governments
concerned accept these price consequences for agricultural commodities, arguing either that lower prices were unacceptable for their
farmers, or that higher prices were inflationary. The following simple
hypothetical example is used to illustrate the nature of these decisions
and the consequences which flowed from them.

Green currency system - hypothetical data
Suppose that initially 1UA = 5DM = 7FF
   1 tonne of wheat is 10UA = 50DM = 70FF
Then the DM is revalued and the FF is devalued, so that
1UA = 4DM = 8FF
but for agriculture the old exchange rates are retained.
Diagramatically:

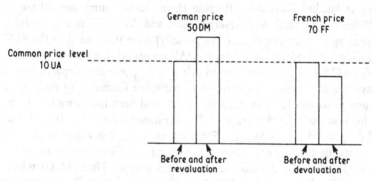

Figure 4.1   The effects of exchange rate alterations on real values.

Because the *real* values of DMs and FFs have changed, the prices of
wheat per tonne in Germany and France *should* have become 40DM
and 80FF respectively. Preservation of the original national prices
requires the use of artificial exchange rates; these are officially
termed *representative* rates although their association with agriculture
has led them to be known universally as 'green rates'.

In the early 1970s other currencies began to change in value and the
system of fixed exchange rates slowly disintegrated. In August 1971
the US dollar's convertibility into gold was ended, and the dollar, like

many other currencies, floated. Floating means that a currency's exchange rate is determined by market forces and may therefore change from time to time. The CAP's price-support system had developed during a time of fixed exchange rates and assumed the continuation of such stability. Floating rates implied the necessity continually to revise agricultural prices in terms of national currencies because the values of national currencies were always changing relative to the still constant UA. Consequently, as an administrative convenience national agricultural prices were calculated from UA prices at still fixed rates of exchange just as described for the mark and franc changes discussed above. These 'green' rates were changed occasionally towards the rates determined in the currency markets, so that they did not get too far from reality.

In 1973 certain EEC currencies were stabilized by means of a joint-float, that is the monetary authorities of the countries concerned co-operated to keep the values of their currencies within previously agreed limits. The UA for agricultural purposes was redefined in terms of these 'snake' currencies. Because these 'snake' currencies (those of Belgium, Luxembourg, Netherlands and West Germany mainly, although others participated temporarily) were stronger than the EEC average, the agricultural UA (AUA) gradually appreciated. By 1978 the AUA had thus increased in value by 21 per cent compared to the average of Community currencies. For some Community purposes a new European Unit of Account (EUA) had been introduced in 1975; this was a weighted average of all Community currencies. In 1979 the European Monetary System (EMS) was introduced in a further attempt to stabilize exchange rates (comprising all Community members except the UK); it used the European Currency Unit (ECU) which was defined to equal the EUA. Now the point of immediate concern in this complicated story is that the AUA has since 1979 been the ECU; but noting that the AUA had appreciated by 21 per cent compared to the ECU (= EUA), all agricultural prices were increased by 21 per cent in terms of the ECU – that is agricultural prices kept the 21 per cent gain in real terms due to the appreciation of the units in which they had been denominated. (Appendix 4.1 details ECUs and green rates in 1982.)

Monetary Compensatory Amounts

Now that the complicated digression on the nature and history of agricultural units of account has been completed it would be as well to return to the green currencies example above. The situation reached was that despite revaluations and devaluations the original UA exchange rates had been retained for agricultural purposes. This example is now continued using the same data:

Green rates of exchange 1UA = 5DM = 7FF
Market rates of exchange 1UA = 4DM = 8FF
Price of wheat = 10UA/tonne = 50DM = 70FF (at green rates)

Suppose a German importer purchased 1 tonne of wheat in France for 70FF, he could sell it in Germany for 50DM. But at the market rate of exchange 1FF = ½ DM, so at 70FF the wheat would have cost him only 35DM. Clearly (assuming for simplicity of exposition no transport costs), all French wheat would soon be in Germany under such circumstances. To prevent this, prices need to be equalized in real terms – the French wheat entering Germany has to pay a tax of 15DM to FEOGA. Similarly, agricultural commodities exported from Germany where prices are high are subject to a subsidy from FEOGA to reduce them to the price levels of France or whichever other Community country they are bound for. These border taxes and subsidies are termed Monetary Compensatory Amounts (MCAs).

From the example it is plain that green currencies result in different real prices in EC member countries. MCAs permit agricultural commodities to be traded between the countries as though common prices existed (as they were intended under the Treaty of Rome). However, the single market, one of the three basic principles of the CAP, is no more than a fiction, a mirage created and maintained by MCAs.

Uncommon prices

At this point it is necessary to remember the economic rationale of a common market – that free trade within those countries should result in each commodity being produced where it can be made or grown most efficiently. The removal of trade barriers which previously prevented this thus ultimately increases the economic well-being of all the participants. Clearly, the MCA system of border taxes and subsidies operates entirely contrary to the principles of a common market – indeed, one system of trade barriers has been substituted for another. The significance of this is a matter of degree: if MCAs are small, meaning that price differences are slight, then little has been lost.

Table 4.1 gives prices for three commodities for 1978. These three commodities have been chosen because they are of uniform quality and so more easily compared than for example the meats. The year 1978 was chosen as the first year after the end of the transitional period for the three new members; hence the single market stage of common prices should have been achieved. The table demonstrates clearly that the real price differences between countries were very considerable. Writing about this situation in the 1970s Koester (1978, 7) said that if MCAs were regarded as customs duties (which they are in the sense that they prevent trade flows which would otherwise lead to equal prices), then 'trade restrictions within the EEC are currently greater than is permitted according to GATT rules .... What we now have in the EEC is not a customs union'. (GATT, the General Agreement on Tariffs and Trade, governs international trade in the free world.) At the time of writing (1983) there has been little change in this situation.

Having shown that agricultural price differences between EEC countries are very large, it is necessary to consider the consequences. Two are particularly important. First, competition between countries is distorted; second, national contributions to and receipts from FEOGA are affected. This latter financial matter is considered in Chapter 6. Here we concentrate on the competition aspect.

The Treaty of Rome is clear and specific in its attitude to competition. In Article 3 the EEC is pledged to 'the establishment of a

Table 4.1 Farmers' selling prices of certain commodities in 1978

	ECU per 100 kg		
	Soft wheat	Eggs	Butter
Germany	18.00	6.22	312.82
France	13.87	5.84	287.64
Italy	17.09	4.98	256.26
Netherlands	16.18	3.86	285.39
Belgium	16.55	3.54	288.13
Luxembourg	15.88	—	352.66
UK	13.15	3.19	214.10
Ireland	14.76	4.52	253.18
Denmark	15.54	5.30	272.81

Source: Statistical Office of the EC (1981)

system ensuring that competition shall not be distorted in the Common Market'. Thus the existence of widely different national agricultural price levels due to the operation of the CAP is incompatible with the Treaty. This distortion of competition between farmers may be unfair, but its implications for industrial competition are more serious even if only because the industrial sector is so much larger than the agricultural sector. Clearly the prices of agricultural produce at wholesale, which is the stage of marketing affected by the CAP, will influence retail food prices. Food prices are generally believed to be important influences upon industrial wages. Thus it is possible that the widely differing CAP price levels which have been demonstrated are in themselves significantly distorting industrial competition.

Green currencies and national policies

Representative rates of exchange and market rates may diverge considerably; there is no automatic mechanism towards convergence. A national government may *decide* to alter its green rate towards the market rate and be allowed to do so by its Community partners, but a government's power of veto prevents the Council *forcing* a change in rate. Similarly, a change away from the market rate of exchange would not be agreed. Thus a government can allow its representative rate of exchange to remain substantially different from its market rate if in the government's judgement this is in the national interest (disregarding the interests of the Community as a whole!).

There are several reasons why divergences between green and market rates of exchange may suit a government. To illustrate the case for an overvalued green currency the example of sterling may be used. During the Labour administration of 1974-9 the green pound was considerably overvalued – at some times by as much as 30 per cent. This was because the market rate of exchange of sterling had fallen, and although the representative rate of exchange had been altered towards the market rate, these alterations had been too small to equalize the rates. CAP prices were constant in terms of UAs, so, if the green pound was overvalued by 30 per cent it meant that the prices of agricultural products in the UK were kept 30 per cent below the levels which would have ruled if the green pound had equalled the market rate of exchange. This policy thus kept food prices down, and was greatly favoured by the British government which was at the time presiding over record British inflation rates. Of course the policy had disadvantages to offset relatively cheap food. Farmers' incomes were reduced (and the CAP is supposed to be for their benefit) and consequently so were their investments and output. It follows that food imports were increased and the UK's balance of trade damaged; this added to the pressures reducing the value of the pound which resulted in the green pound being overvalued.

Deutschmarks provide the example of an undervalued green currency. It was noted earlier that after the 1969 revaluation of the mark the CAP representative rate for marks was not changed because such a change would have reduced agricultural prices in Germany. Thus German farmers have enjoyed high prices, as indicated in Table 4.1. Concomitantly German consumers have paid high prices for food, and farm output has been encouraged.

To sum up, governments may use green currencies to reinforce national policies by delaying adjustments when market exchange rates alter. Such use of green currencies has become so widespread that major agricultural price differences exist between countries within the EEC.

Attempts to regain common prices: removal of MCAs

In 1978 agricultural prices in the UK were about 30 per cent below the 'common' level fixed in ECUs, whereas German farmers enjoyed prices more than 10 per cent above the 'common' level; these were the extremes of the prices spread. The Commission was dismayed by these huge price differences and tried to encourage member states to phase out MCAs, that is to re-align green currency rates with market rates and thus return to common prices. At this time the EMS was being set up, and France proposed that when CAP prices were denominated in ECUs it should be on the basis that 1ECU = 1AUA. As discussed above, the AUA had appreciated by 21 per cent against the average of the Community currencies so that this proposal implied a 21 per cent reduction in agricultural prices in real terms. France further proposed that MCAs should be frozen at their existing levels and then gradually phased out. Acceptance of these proposals would have given French farmers a larger share of the market by reducing output in higher-cost countries, notably Germany. However, Germany refused to agree to such changes, because of the substantial reduction in German farm prices which was entailed. Consequently France blocked the introduction of the EMS (due for 1 January 1979) until March 1979 when a new agreement on MCAs was negotiated. This accepted the denomination of CAP prices in ECUs increased by 21 per cent to allow for the difference in value between ECUs and AUAs, and promised that increases in MCAs due to *new* divergencies between green currencies and market rates of exchange would be phased out within two years. However, nothing was agreed about the removal of *existing* MCAs.

Economic and Monetary Union

Divergencies in real agricultural prices between member states have arisen because of currency fluctuations; as noted earlier, the CAP system assumed the existence of fixed exchange rates. There is only one way in which common agricultural prices can be truly common within the existing CAP: that is if there was one common currency replacing all national currencies. This is one of the fundamental objectives of moves towards economic and monetary union (EMU). The price problems of the CAP are by no means the only justification for EMU, indeed the issues involved are far wider. Most of the arguments are outside the scope of this book, but they will be outlined here in order to indicate the likely future for EMU and hence for common prices with the existing CAP mechanisms.

There are two fundamentally different approaches towards European unity; one is based upon the principle of co-operation without the surrender of national sovereignty. In contrast the federalist approach is to surrender a significant degree of national sovereignty to international institutions. As discussed in Chapter 3, the EEC was founded by governments which were largely federalist. The Rome Treaty shows this clearly by stating in several articles that decisions in the first stages of the implementation of the Treaty should be by unanimous vote but subsequently by qualified majority voting – 'qualified' here meaning that the votes are weighted taking into account the size of the country, with 12 constituting a majority. The original weights (Article 147) are as follows:

Belgium	2	Germany	4	France	4
Italy	4	Luxembourg	1	Netherlands	2

In practice EEC members sought to protect their national interests so that qualified majority voting failed to become the normal method for decision-taking. Indeed, under the Luxembourg Compromise of 1966, discussed in Chapter 3, a country could veto any decision which it declared to be against its national interest. Thus the unanimity principle became of fundamental importance.

In the 1960s Community progress towards unity through co-operation was less than many had hoped. The attitude of General de Gaulle who favoured a 'Europe des Patries' had been paramount. However, when the General resigned the federalist motive again came to the fore. Thus the Hague Summit of 1969 aimed towards integration as well as agreeing to the objective of enlarging the Community. EMU was the chosen form of integration adopted.

Ultimately EMU implied on the political side the surrender of national sovereignty to some Community authority in matters which affected all members, including defence. On the economic side new Community institutions would control monetary policy, taxation, the budget, balance of payments and so on. Of particular importance to the CAP, currencies would become freely convertible at fixed rates of exchange, possibly to be superseded by a new European currency unit. There are numerous arguments in favour of EMU. Politically, such a united Europe would be a powerful force for peace and democracy in the world. Economically, EMU is the logical step following the completion of a customs union. As can be seen for the CAP, the proper functioning of common policies would be more completely achieved. In general, increased economic integration would bring about more rapid economic growth, strengthening the Community. However, if one country became less competitive than other members, it would just become relatively poorer, lacking the ability to alter its situation through economic measures appropriate to its particular situation. So the more efficient and prosperous areas of the Community would grow at the expense of the poorer and less efficient areas. Just as the South East of England has become more prosperous than the North East, so the UK as a whole, for example, might become a depressed region relative to continental Europe.

Progress towards EMU was cut short by the currency problems of the 1970s. However, in the long run it is a lack of political will which is likely to prevent progress in the foreseeable future. The 1973 enlargement of the Community has made political integration more difficult; the accession of Greece in 1981 and further prospective enlargements will surely add to the difficulties.

Conclusion

The basic requirements of a common market are common prices and the free movement of goods between member countries. These features are absent from the Community's agricultural sector. Agricultural price differences between member countries are very large indeed; they are allowed to persist through the use of specially introduced trade barriers – monetary compensatory amounts (MCAs). Price differences of the order which have existed since 1969 distort competition between member countries and reduce the economic benefits which should be achieved through intra-Community free trade.

Within the EEC the MCA system has been used by member states with national rather than Community interests in mind and with scant regard for the economic rationale of a customs union. If politicians are unable to achieve the agreed goal of common agricultural prices, the chances of their embracing more advanced measures of integration such as economic and monetary union are remote indeed. So common prices seem unattainable either directly through the abolition of MCAs or indirectly through further economic integration.

In the face of major internal price differences and trade barriers it must be concluded that the CAP as it has operated since 1969 is not compatible with the principles of a common market.

Appendix 4.1   Units of account

Since 1962 the Community has used its own currency units in preference to the alternative of any particular national currency. At first, the unit of account (UA) was defined in terms of gold – 0.88867088 grammes, exactly the same amount as one US dollar before the latter was devalued in 1971.

From 1969 onwards the fixed exchange rate system fell into disorder as exchange rates of various currencies began to alter. Many currencies were floated in 1971 and most have floated ever since. In 1972 the EEC members attempted to stabilize their currencies by co-operating in exchange markets; this joint float of currencies moving together is termed the 'snake'. This operation met with mixed success in that some currencies were stabilized but others were forced out of the snake by large changes in their parity. In 1975 the European Unit of Account

(EUA) was introduced for certain purposes, notably the European Development Fund. This was a weighted basket of all EEC currencies. Throughout these changes, the Community budget used the original UA, but this was replaced by the EUA in 1978. In 1979 a new European Currency Unit (ECU) was introduced; this was equal in value to the EUA and is now used for budgetary purposes.

The ECU is defined as a weighted basket of EEC currencies, the weights being approximately proportional to GNPs. In 1982 it was made up as follows:

BFR 3.66, LFR 0.14, HFL 0.286, DKR 0.217, DM 0.828, LIT 109, FF 1.15, UKL 0.0885, IRL 0.00759

Under the Act of Accession the Greek drachma is due to be included by the end of 1985.

AGRICULTURAL UNITS OF ACCOUNT

When exchange rates began to alter in 1969 the common prices of agricultural products were of course denominated in UAs. Members whose currencies changed value in relation to the UA did not for a variety of reasons wish to change their agricultural prices immediately in terms of national currencies although all other sectors of their economies had to make such adjustments. Instead they retained their previously existing agricultural prices in terms of their own currencies, converting these into UAs at special fixed 'representative' or 'green' rates of exchange; this necessitated the use of monetary compensatory amounts (MCAs) on imports and exports between member states. In 1973 the UA for agricultural purposes was redefined in terms of the 'snake' currencies and the agricultural unit of account (AUA) gradually appreciated in value. In 1979 the AUA was replaced by the ECU, but was by then worth almost 21 per cent more than the ECU. It was accordingly decided that to prevent consequential changes in agricultural prices a coefficient of 1.208953 should be applied to all common prices and green rates in converting them from AUAs to ECUs.

Table Appendix 4.1.1 gives the values of national currencies and green currencies in terms of ECUs to demonstrate the differences between them. Similarly, Figure Appendix 4.1.1. shows for one currency how green rates are gradually moved towards market rates of exchange but rarely manage to get there.

Table Appendix 4.1.1   Values of national currencies and green rates in terms of ECUs

	Values in national currencies of one ECU 31 August 1982	Representative rates (green rates) July–August 1982
Belgian franc and Luxembourg franc (convertible)	45.1920	42.9772
Belgian franc and Luxembourg franc (financial)	47.7157	
German mark	2.35866	2.57524[1]
		2.65660[2]
Dutch guilder	2.58226	2.75563[1]
		2.81318[2]
Pound sterling	0.549484	0.618655
Danish krone	8.23409	8.23400
French franc	6.62690	6.19564
Italian lira	1 327.69	1 289.00[4]
		1 258.00[5]
		1 227.00[2]
Irish pound	0.685907	0.691011
Greek drachma	66.8162	64.8597[3]
		66.5526[2]

Source: ECC (1982d)

Notes: [1]For sugar and isoglucose, milk and milk products, beef and veal, sheepmeat, and (in August) for cereals, eggs and poultrymeat
[2]For other products
[3]For dried grapes and olive oil
[4]For sugar and isoglucose, milk and milk products, beef and veal, sheepmeat, wine and seeds
[5]For pigmeat, olive oil and fish

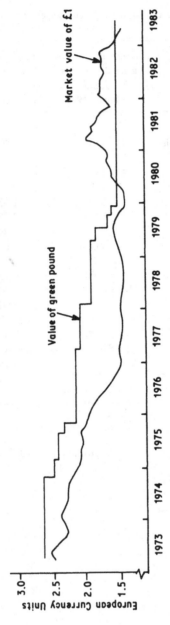

Figure Appendix 4.1.1 The changing fortunes of the green pound. The green pound was overvalued from its introduction in February 1973 until the spring of 1980. At the end of 1976 this overvaluation reached its maximum and resulted in an MCA of −45 per cent. Conversely the green pound has been undervalued during the 1980s until 1983. The maximum positive MCA was 18.2 per cent achieved in February 1981. Such large MCAs are effective intra-Community trade barriers.

5 Mountains and lakes: the problem of surpluses

Butter and beef mountains and lakes of wine are the sensational scenery of newspaper headlines. This chapter considers the causes of these and other common market surpluses and the problems to which they give rise. Milk, the most intractable surplus product, is examined to show the difficulties and costs of getting rid of or preventing surpluses. One major method of disposal is by export at subsidized prices, and the costs of this to the Community, and to both consuming and competing countries, is discussed. Finally an attempt is made to assess the importance of both the financial and economic costs of surpluses to the Community.

Agricultural progress and surpluses

The agricultural sectors of the Community countries, in common with those of the other industrialized countries of Western Europe and North America, have developed dramatically in the years since the Second World War. These developments have been characterized by very high rates of growth of output resulting from technological advances, the replacement of labour by machinery and a gradual increase in farm size. Included in the term 'technological advance' is the genetic improvement of crops and livestock, the introduction of many new pesticides and herbicides, improvements in machinery and the growing ability of farmers to apply new techniques.

Increased crop and livestock yields are the most obvious evidence of technological progress. Their spectacular growth for the Nine is indicated by data given in Table 5.1 for some of the major commodities. As the area of land used for agriculture has remained virtually constant the rising yields are reflected in total output.

The populations of West European countries have long enjoyed high enough incomes to be well fed, so when incomes increase further

Table 5.1 Yields of certain agricultural products in the Nine

	100 kg/ha					milk kg/cow
	wheat	barley	maize	potatoes	sugar beet	
1955	23.3	26.8	25.4	172.7	332.5	na
1960	23.9	30.5	32.9	198.0	425.4	2943
1965	29.9	33.3	35.5	207.5	375.3	3134
1970	31.8	31.3	49.2	245.5	408.1	3448
1973	38.2	38.8	55.4	268.1	441.0	3582
1974	40.3	39.9	48.9	285.5	399.9	3599
1975	36.3	35.9	47.4	243.1	405.7	3665
1976	34.9	33.6	47.4	211.6	411.6	3762
1977	38.2	39.8	57.1	271.1	450.3	3846
1978	43.3	41.5	57.5	291.1	433.4	3962
1979	47.5	41.5	57.5	292.0	435.0	4041
1980+	44.5	39.9	57.3	285.0	458.0	4073

Sources: Statistical Office of the EC (1980) *Land Use and Production*; *Yearbook of Agricultural Statistics*, various years; Milk Marketing Board *EC Dairy Facts and Figures*, various years

Notes: +Data include Greece

little extra is spent on food. Even what extra is spent tends to be on extra processing or packaging rather than quantity. Population growth is slight. It follows that food consumption has increased relatively little in recent years although production has been rising rapidly. For many agricultural products output has exceeded consumption. The situation is summarized in Table 5.2. which shows self-sufficiency ratios gradually increasing as output has outpaced consumption.

Agriculture's contribution to economic development was examined in detail in Chapter 1. One central aspect is of interest in the present context: when the supply of agricultural commodities grows more rapidly than demand, prices fall; lower food prices increase the real incomes of consumers but they also mean lower earnings for agricultural resources, so that some, notably labour, leave agriculture to be used in some other economic sector. All this presupposes a free market and so does not apply in the EEC. Indeed the fundamental basis of the CAP is price support to help maintain farmers' incomes. Thus the CAP attempts in some measure to stem the tide of economic development. In a free market prices equilibrate the opposing forces of

Table 5.2 Self-sufficiency ratios, major agricultural commodities

	Wheat	Barley	Maize	Sugar	Potatoes	Wine	Butter	Beef	Pork	Eggs
1956-60 (6)	90	84	64	104	101	89	101	92	100	90
1972 (6)	111	110	68	122	101	95	124	81	99	99
1972 (9)	99	102	58	100	100	93	106	84	100	99
1974 (9)	107	103	59	92	100	115	93	100	100	100
1976 (9)	101	103	53	105	98	98	107	99	99	100
1978 (9)	102	112	58	125	101	93	118	95	100	101
1978 (10)	103	111	56	123	101	95	118	94	100	101
1980 (10)	114	111	62	125	101	112	120	103	100	101

Source: Statistical Office of the EC *Yearbook of Agricultural Statistics*, various years
Notes: Figures in parentheses indicate the size of the Community to which the data
refer. Looking at 1972 it will be noted that the self-sufficiency ratios for the
Nine are mostly lower than for the Six; this is due to the UK's large net import
requirement for many foodstuffs. The 1978 figures respectively exclude and
include Greece; clearly the latter's accession alters the picture very little.

supply and demand: if supply exceeds demand prices fall, increasing
consumption and discouraging supplies until quantities demanded and
supplied are equal. Under the CAP prices cannot fall below
intervention levels; hence there is no equilibrating mechanism as
supplies increase and output can chronically exceed consumption. The
amount by which output exceeds consumption is termed a surplus.
This is not the only definition of surplus but is the sense in which it is
usually used in an EEC context.

Returning to Table 5.2 and the self-sufficiency ratios for 1980 it can
be seen that the EEC is more that self-sufficient in several major
commodities. In that year 25 per cent more sugar was produced than
was consumed, and significant surpluses of other major products also
existed. Maize is the only product shown for which there is a large
import requirement. This commodity is used mainly as an animal
feeding stuff, in which category most of the EEC's temperate zone
agricultural imports fall; of course the EEC is also a major importer of
many tropical agricultural products such as coffee.

Surpluses can be classified into two main groups, seasonal and
structural. A seasonal surplus exists when output temporarily exceeds
consumption. For most commodities, such as wheat, for which there
is one harvest but consumption throughout the year, a seasonal surplus
thus defined is virtually certain to occur. The CAP deals with these by

varying the support prices during the year sufficiently to induce storage. For some commodities a seasonal surplus may occur in the sense that exceptionally favourable production conditions lead to an unexpected surge in output. This happened to wine in two of the years shown in Table 5.2. Beef has also been occasionally in surplus. The intervention authorities purchase such surpluses for sale at a later date when output is lower. Such an activity helps to stabilize prices for the benefit of both producers and consumers.

A structural surplus occurs when output exceeds consumption. Table 5.2 shows that this is the situation for cereals, sugar and butter. The intervention authorities purchase these surpluses but have no hope of resale on EEC markets later. Thus stockpiles or 'mountains' of them are accumulated and attract much public attention (their ultimate disposal is considered below). Beef 'mountains' and wine 'lakes' are less frequent and so less serious; they have received an undue share of attention because these luxuries excite the public far more than, for example, cereals.

It is generally considered immoral to destroy food, so this method of disposing of intervention stocks cannot be considered by politicians in a democracy. But there are finite limits to storage capacity, so commodities in chronic surplus have to be disposed of somehow. Two main outlets are used: selling at a low price for animal feed, and exporting with the aid of export subsidies. These are very costly methods of removing surpluses as can be seen in Table 5.3, which shows the costs of price support by commodity for 1980. Financing these costs is the subject of Chapter 6; for the present we note the very large expenditures involved in surplus disposal but return to the surplus problem itself; to explore it further we will examine milk.

Milk surpluses were a frequently met problem in many countries of West Europe before the advent of the EEC. In the Community the milk surplus has been the most intractable, and as the expenditures in Table 5.3 indicate, the most serious of the surpluses. Milk is the single most important product in terms of farm revenue in the Community and it is the mainstay of small farmers in particular (see Table 5.4). So when milk production expanded under the stimulus of technological advance, the income-raising role of the supported price was regarded as paramount, and it could not be reduced to curb output. At the same time the consumption of fresh milk and butter declined, not only because of high prices to consumers but also through competition from relatively cheap 'soft quality' margarines and because of health fears

Table 5.3 FEOGA guarantee expenditure by commodity, 1980

| | Million ECU | | |
	Export subsidies	Intervention	Total
Milk products	2745.9	2006.1	4752.0
Cereals	1174.7	494.3	1669.0
Beef and veal	715.5	647.8	1363.3
Sugar	286.2	289.0	575.2
Oils and fats	3.7	683.6	687.3
Pigmeat	91.6	24.0	115.6
Sheepmeat	—	53.5	53.5
Eggs and poultrymeat	85.5	—	85.5
Fruit and vegetables	41.3	646.0	687.3
Wine	26.4	273.1	299.5
Tobacco	4.5	304.8	309.3
Fishery products	11.4	11.6	23.0
Other intervention products		115.8	115.8
of which:			
Flax and hemp		16.8	
Seed		32.0	
Hops		6.2	
Silkworms		0.3	
Dried fodder		33.5	
Peas and field beans		27.0	
Cotton		—	
Miscellaneous	221.3		221.3
MCAs			298.5
Grand total			11 314.9

Source: ECC (1981c), 245

associated with animal fats. A small increase in the consumption of milk products such as cheese and yoghurt provided little compensation. So dairy product surpluses became a chronic problem which could not be solved by price reductions.

A brief digression is necessary at this point to explain the nature of surplus milk. There are three major components of milk: water (87 to 88 per cent), butterfat (3–4 per cent) and milk proteins and sugar (8–9 per cent). Butter is formed by separating out the butterfat, leaving as a by-product skim milk, which may be dried to give skim milk powder

Table 5.4 Dairy farming in the European Community, 1979

	% farms with dairy cows	Average size of herd	% revenue from milk
Germany	52	11.9	23.0
France	46[a]	14.4	16.7
Italy	17[a]	6.4	10.4
Netherlands	48	31.7	27.8
Belgium	49	16.8	17.5
Luxembourg	60	21.4	43.3
UK	24	52.8	22.5
Ireland	48[b]	14.2	32.3
Denmark	38	23.0	25.4
EC (9)	29	14.0	19.7

Sources: Column 1: Milk Marketing Board *EEC Dairy Facts and Figures*, 1980, 1981; columns 2 and 3: ECC (1981c)
Notes: [a]1977
[b]1975

(SMP). Fresh milk is not convenient to store because of its high water-content and perishability. So to support the milk price, intervention prices are set for butter and SMP. Milk that cannot be sold more profitably as fresh milk or as cheese or other milk products will be made into butter and SMP, and any quantities not bought by consumers are purchased at the intervention prices and stored. Thus the production of surplus milk gives rise to butter and SMP 'mountains'. To give an indication of the size of these mountains, it is estimated that in 1979 they were each about one-quarter of the Community's annual consumption (House of Lords Select Committee 1980, viii).

The prevention and the disposal of surpluses

Prevention is proverbially better than cure, and would mean, in the case of milk, either reducing output and/or expanding the consumption of milk and milk products. Cutting the price of milk would be the most effective way of reducing output, but the CAP is designed to support farmers' incomes by raising prices (alternatives to price support are considered in Chapter 8). Fewer dairy cows should give less milk; the logic of this proposition has been well tested in the EEC, particularly during the early 1970s. FEOGA financed a variety of schemes, the two main ones involving a slaughter premium to dairy farmers to cull some of their cows, and conversion subsidies to those who would switch from dairy to beef cattle. Farmers used the slaughter premiums to improve the quality of their cows, higher-yielding young stock replacing old cows which were ready for slaughter anyway. Beef cattle produce less revenue from a given area of land than dairy cattle, so relatively few EEC dairy farmers are large enough for the desired switch to be feasible. By the end of the 1970s the number of dairy cattle was only slightly reduced, while the total quantity of milk they produced was significantly greater.

In 1977 a 'co-responsibility levy' was introduced. This is a levy on each litre of milk produced and it is intended to reduce surpluses. As the title suggests, milk producers are supposed to share the responsibility for surpluses. In theory the levy is a two-edged sword: firstly it reduces the farmers' milk price and so discourages output, secondly the funds raised are used to promote the sales of milk and milk products. In practice the co-responsibility levy has turned out to be a very blunt instrument on both accounts. As a covert reduction in price it is ineffective because it is too small, and a larger levy would defeat the income-raising objective of the CAP. Sales promotion has so far made no significant inroads into the butter mountain or persuaded consumers sufficiently to expand their requirements for milk in any form. Indeed the consumption of milk and milk products in total is still gradually declining.

Consumer subsidies are another way of increasing consumption, the subsidy reducing the price to consumers. However the CAP's basic method of operation is to raise prices to consumers, so to reduce them again in order to remove the surpluses does not appeal to logical minds. However, consumer subsidies on a small scale (relative to the Community as a whole) have been used, notably in the UK. It was feared that if UK butter prices increased to Community levels too quickly after accession the large UK butter market would decline rapidly and fail to ameliorate the butter surplus problem as much as had been hoped. Therefore a special subsidy has been used to date to keep UK butter prices lower than they would otherwise be under the CAP. In other Community countries butter sales at reduced prices for a brief period at the end of the year have made 'Christmas butter' a new tradition! As noted earlier, the widespread use of consumer subsidies is incompatible with the CAP. One further method of increasing butter consumption is to persuade people who would not otherwise eat butter to do so. This method of 'special sales' at low prices puts butter into the diets of hospital patients, the armed services and students via their refectories. Despite these efforts there remains much surplus butter.

As the milk surplus resists all attempts at prevention, the problem is how to get rid of it. There are two main methods used for surplus disposal under the CAP – denaturing and exporting. Denaturing means changing a product into some form in which it can be used in markets other than the normal high-priced food market, the loss involved being financed by FEOGA. SMP is protein-rich and so can be used in animal feeds; a FEOGA subsidy for this purpose has helped reduce stocks considerably. Some SMP gets into dairy cattle feeds – surely the ultimate in recycling! No effective way of removing butter stocks by denaturing has yet been devised. Exporting butter is the obvious alternative, and as Table 5.3 shows this is done on a considerable scale and at great expense. The difficulty here is not only of expense but of actually finding export markets. When the UK joined the EEC the interests of New Zealand as a major exporter of milk products were catered for by granting her reduced but continued access to the UK market and also by promising not to dump butter on other New Zealand markets. This is implied by paragraph 107 of the 1971 White Paper (HM Government, 1971), part of which says:

> The Community have undertaken to make every effort to promote the conclusion of an international agreement on dairy products; and to pursue a trade policy which will not frustrate New Zealand's efforts to diversify. This should help New Zealand to increase her earnings in other markets.

Hence the Community has sold large quantities of butter to Russia – not a traditional outlet for New Zealand's or anyone else's butter. These sales have been strongly criticized, particularly by British politicians and press, who complain that butter is sold to Russia at 'knock-down' prices, certainly well below butter prices in UK shops. Economists used to illustrate the choices facing society by saying that a country could have either guns *or* butter; wags now observe that thanks to the EEC Russia can have guns *and* butter.

An extra outlet for SMP is to use it as food aid, i.e. give it away or sell it on particularly favourable terms to countries which are short of food. Because it is protein-rich, SMP is an especially valuable supplement to the diets of children in areas struck by famine. Being a powder, SMP is relatively cheap to transport and easily stored. Butter mountains cannot be used for food aid because butter does not normally feature in Third World diets and its need for refrigerated transport makes it impracticable; it is not of fundamental nutritional value anyway.

This excursion into milk surplus problems can be extended briefly to see how the other surpluses are tackled. Only one other product has a form of co-responsibility levy – sugar. Since the inception of a common sugar policy in 1968 production beyond a certain level has been subject to a levy. The sugar levy is one source of income for the Community. Denaturing is practised with several products. Thus sugar is offered to bee-keepers who need sugar to give their bees to replace the honey removed. Such sugar is contaminated with garlic (as a beekeeper the author accepts that the bees may not mind the garlic, but sugar and garlic stores left in the hive at the end of winter may become mixed with the new season's honey!). This is not a major outlet. Wheat is sold cheaply for animal feed, having been tainted with fish oil so that it will not re-enter the higher priced milling market for bread flour. Some surplus wine has been distilled to produce industrial alcohol. significant quantities of wheat have been disposed of as food aid. Disposal by export subsidy remains the major outlet for Community surpluses.

Subsidized food exports and third countries

An outline of this topic is necessary because it is one of the sources of pressure for reform of the CAP. Two elements of the CAP are important in the world context: the raising and the stabilizing of agricultural prices within the EEC. These have substantial effects on third countries because the EEC is the world's largest single importer of agricultural products and a major exporter also. High prices within the EEC increase agricultural production and restrict consumption; therefore agricultural imports are reduced because of the CAP and exports are increased. Reduced markets within the EEC countries because of the CAP have long been an irritant to the agricultural exporting countries. The dumping of large quantities of agricultural surpluses on world markets naturally infuriates the low-cost producers of such countries. Thus wheat is produced more cheaply than in the

EEC by Argentina, Australia, Canada and the United States of America, yet these countries' outputs have to compete on world markets with EEC wheat sold at prices much below EEC costs of production. New Zealand butter is the ultimate example: it can be produced in that distant place and transported to Europe at a cost far below the export subsidy given to EEC butter. From the point of view of other agricultural exporting countries the problem is of excess and access – the EEC dumps its excess on to world markets and denies access to its own markets. The excess aspect of complaints is obviously justified but the Commission frequently emphasizes that despite access complaints the Community's imports of agricultural products continue to expand. By implication access is not restricted unduly. Superficially, this argument appears to be valid, for as Table 5.5 shows, the EEC's net imports of agricultural products have been increasing, at least until 1978. A closer scrutiny of the data in this table reveals two opposing trends: first, imports of food products increased following the accession of the UK but then began to decline markedly under the

Table 5.5 European Community net imports of agricultural products, 1974–80

| | million ECU | | | |
	1974	1976	1978	1980
Food products	8141	12 522	12 464	10 246
of which: Cereals	1525	2 395	559	− 939
Beef and veal	164	78	149	− 283
Beverages and tobacco	− 369	− 585	− 859	− 1 493
Skins and furs	617	908	793	1 012
Oil seeds	2465	2 442	2 952	3 246
Natural rubber	487	516	542	765
Timber and cork	3250	3 607	3 863	5 600
Natural textile fibres	1795	2 182	1 990	2 149
Agricultural raw materials	209	245	301	322
Oils and fats	1204	683	820	862
Starches and gluten	5	− 17	− 26	− 18
Totals	17 804	22 504	22 840	22 691

Source: Derived from ECC *The Agricultural Situation in the Community*, various years
Note: Negatives indicate net exports

influence of CAP-induced surpluses for some commodities; second, the opposite trend is displayed by products which are not covered by the CAP, the rubber and timber of which the Community has a 'natural' deficit. So, as one would expect, the data support the contention that the CAP restricts access; indeed it is remarkable that anyone should attempt to disguise such obvious facts.

Turning to the question of price stability, it is evident that the intervention system is designed for and does promote stable prices. These in turn mean that the Community's consumption of agricultural produce is also stable. In marked contrast the output of agricultural produce is very unstable, influenced as it is by the weather and by pests and diseases. In conjunction, stable consumption and unstable production mean that, for many commodities, EEC import requirements or export availabilities fluctuate considerably from year to year. Because of its major part in world markets these fluctuating dealings by the EEC are a destabilizing influence. World commodity prices are inherently unstable; their further destabilization by the EEC is undesirable and must be harmful to other countries that are more dependent than the Community on food exports.

Virtually all the major agricultural exporting countries have complained vociferously about the trade effects of the CAP. Their feelings are probably accurately summed up by the US Secretary of State for Agriculture who in 1981 said that the US was 'willing to try almost anything to convince the Community to change its agricultural subsidies policy which was threatening the world trading system' (quoted in Pearce 1981, 121). In 1982 the US threatened retaliatory measures which, if carried out, could signal the start of a very damaging trade war. One particular threat is to sell the American butter surplus to Russia, pre-empting EEC sales; the EEC would then have a mountain of butter with no known major market.

In 1982 there were several disputes proceeding within the General Agreement on Tariffs and Trade (GATT) which involved the EEC. Five of these complaints were made in 1981 by the USA; they relate to subsidized EEC exports of wheat flour, poultrymeat, pasta, canned fruit and dried citrus fruits. Also in 1982 complaints against the EEC's sugar export policy were made by the USA, Australia, Brazil and eight developing countries. A counter complaint was made by the EEC against US sugar import quotas and export subsidies. These public signs of behind-the-scenes discord underline the increasingly expressed opinion that trade chaos is imminent.

Costs of the CAP

So far this chapter has detailed the growth of agricultural surpluses despite many varied efforts to prevent them, and has indicated that the costs of their disposal have been substantial. The remainder of the chapter focuses attention on the costs of the CAP. Usually most attention is devoted to the budgetary costs which are associated with surplus disposal, but it will be shown that these are in fact only a minor part of the total costs of the CAP to the Community.

THE BUDGETARY COSTS OF THE CAP

These costs are detailed in Table 5.6. In the early 1960s the main item, the expenditure by FEOGA's Guarantee Section, was small, but it grew rapidly up to 1970, reflecting the introduction of the CAP, commodity by commodity. In 1971, bad weather reduced output and hence the size of surpluses for disposal and their associated expenditures. Since then the trend of guarantee costs has been upwards as output has continued to grow more rapidly than consumption. By comparison the expenditure of the Guidance Sector of FEOGA has been modest and in most years well below the ceilings set.

It is clear that the CAP involves very large budgetary costs, but then the Community is large and these costs have to be seen in perspective. The Commission has attempted this by relating the costs to GNP, showing that they are just less than half of 1 per cent. In fact this makes them appear less significant than they are; it is more realistic to look at them in terms of their consequences or the alternative uses of the finances. The table shows that FEOGA expenditures are generally about three-quarters of the total Community budget. Since the total budget is limited by the 'own resources' system the size of the CAP share leaves relatively little for anything else. Thus one consequence of the high-cost CAP is that the development of other Community policies is stifled.

In the early years of the EEC the economic gain offered by the formation of a customs union was much discussed; during the UK accession negotiations the economic benefits of joining the Community were heavily emphasized. These gains were generally assessed as being ½ to 1 per cent of GNP (Johnson 1958; Welmesfelder 1960). One can only conclude that if these gains are worthwhile, then the budgetary costs of the CAP must be of major significance.

Table 5.6 FEOGA and total budget expenditure, 1968–80

million ECU

	1968	1969	1970	1971	1972	1973	1974	1975	1976	1977	1978	1979	1980
Guarantee	815.6	1,876.6	2,287.4	1,219.4	3,948.8	3,174.2	3,277.9	4,821.4	5,365.0	6,166.8	8,672.8	10,434.5	11,306.2
Guidance	37.6	24.6	79.4	105.1	74.0	123.7	128.4	184.3	218.2	296.7	428.5	403.4	601.3
Total FEOGA	853.2	1,901.2	2,366.8	1,324.5	4,022.8	3,297.9	3,406.3	5,005.7	5,583.2	6,463.5	9,101.3	10,837.9	11,907.5
Total budget	1,043.7	2,109.9	2,585.5	1,668.9	4,517.7	4,004.6	4,516.4	6,411.2	7,287.6	8,704.9	12,181.7	14,372.4	16,289.1
Guarantee as % total	78.1	88.9	88.5	73.1	87.4	79.3	72.6	75.2	73.6	70.8	71.2	72.6	69.4
FEOGA as % total	81.7	90.1	91.6	79.4	89.0	82.4	75.4	78.1	76.6	74.2	74.7	75.4	73.1

Sources: 1968–78: House of Lords Select Committee (1980); *1979–80*: Statistical Office of the EC (1982)

THE COST OF THE CAP TO CONSUMERS

The essence of the CAP is that it raises the prices of agricultural products at wholesale level. Thus consumers have to pay higher prices for their food than they would if imports were freely permitted. How much the CAP costs consumers depends on the degree by which prices are raised. Table 5.7 shows that EEC prices are much higher than those ruling in world markets, in fact they are generally about double world prices. It is tempting to conclude that the Community's consumers are paying twice as much as is necessary for food, but this does not necessarily follow. Many would argue that if the EEC allowed free trade in agricultural products so that agricultural prices fell to world levels, the Community's agricultural output would be drastically reduced and substantial imports would occur, forcing world prices to rise. This argument is clearly well founded; the big question concerns the extent of the world price rise which extra imports would induce. No precise answer is possible; indeed estimation would be a mammoth undertaking – including, for example, how much the higher prices would cause other importers to reduce imports, which depends *inter alia* on how much their own agricultural industries would respond to the stimulus of higher prices.

If the EEC did substantially reduce agricultural prices, decreasing output and necessitating significant imports, the main products affected would be cereals, sugar, beef and milk. Lower cereal prices would result in lower costs and hence lower prices for pig and poultry meats and eggs; cereals are less important but still significant in the costs of milk and beef production. Clearly cereals are the key product. Could the EEC significantly increase cereal imports without inducing a major rise in world prices? Almost certainly the answer is yes. With the exception of the commodity price boom period 1973–4 and the immediately ensuing years while stocks were rebuilt, there has been a chronic surplus of wheat production capacity in the major exporting countries. The USA is notable in this respect, accounting for one-third to one-half of world wheat exports throughout the 1970s. To prevent world wheat prices falling the USA has been curbing production since the 1950s. It is probable that America would be happy to increase sales at current world prices; considerable expansion in output could be easily achieved. It is worth noting in this context that in 1982 the Americans earned the disapprobation of the EEC by attempting to block member states' 'technological' exports to Russia for the Russian

Table 5.7 Agricultural prices in the EEC as a percentage of world prices

	1967-8	1968-9	1969-70	1970-1	1971-2	1972-3	1973-4	1974-5	1975-6	1976-7	1977-8	1978-9	1979-80	1980-1
Soft wheat	185	195	214	189	209	153	79	107	124	204	216	193	163	146
Hard wheat	200	214	230	231	254	181	116	120	145	236	218	216	159	138
Rice	117	138	186	210	205	115	60	81	137	179	128	157	131	100
Barley	160	197	203	146	185	137	96	107	117	147	206	225	161	134
Maize	160	178	159	141	176	143	98	106	128	163	203	201	190	147
Sugar	438	456	298	203	151	127	66	41	109	176	255	276	134	85
Beef	175	169	147	140	133	112	110	162	196	192	196	199	204	190
Pork+	147	153	137	134	131	147	131	109	113	125	137	155	152	135
Butter	397	504	613	481	171	249	320	316	320	401	388	403	411	286
Olive oil	166	173	167	165	153	125	96	113	207	192	211	200	187	214
Oil seeds	200	203	155	131	147	131	77	80	127	121	153	161	185	168

Source: Statistical Office of the EC Yearbook of Agricultural Statistics, various years
Notes: + After the first two years pork prices are on a calendar year basis
1969/70 shown relates to 1969

gas pipe line, but refused to consider withholding wheat supplies. 'Humanitarian reasons' were given as an excuse but it was well known that the USA was desperately keen to get rid of wheat in the large quantities required by Russia. To round off the argument, the world butter market has suffered a chronic surplus situation for many years, and frequent sugar surpluses have deterred output-increasing investments in developing countries. The question is hypothetical and the answer crude, but the conclusion is that the EEC could import much extra food without causing more than a small rise in world price levels. Pearce (1981, 56) reaches the same conclusion.

For illustrative purposes, assume that the EEC is able to import food at world prices, so that consumers are paying prices approximately double those of the world market as a result of the CAP. Figure 5.1 shows the current situation. Transfers from consumers to producers are represented by area A – the extra cost of food at EEC rather than world prices. The cost of surplus disposal, area B, represents the guarantee section of FEOGA. Since surpluses are only a few per cent of total output it is obvious that area A is several times larger than area B. Clearly, the costs of FEOGA – the budgetary costs of the CAP – which excite so much attention, are merely the tip of the iceberg; consumer transfers are very much larger. One attempt, by Buckwell *et al.* (1982, 168), to measure the costs of the CAP to consumers (area A) for 1980 concludes that they are about double the budgetary costs of

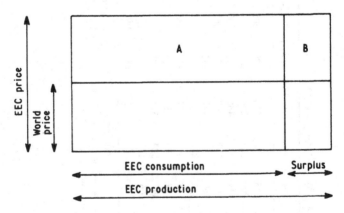

Figure 5.1　Relative costs of the CAP to consumers and to FEOGA. Area A is the extra cost of food to consumers as a result of the CAP; area B is the cost to FEOGA of surplus disposal.

the CAP (area B). This low estimate of consumer costs results from the authors calculating a mere one-third decrease in EEC prices under free trade conditions, an estimate with which the present writer does not agree, as the earlier discussion indicates. Morris (1980, 17) also estimates the consumer transfers to be lower than the present discussion suggests although higher than those of Buckwell *et al*. For cereals, Roberts and Tie (1982) estimate consumer transfers to be six times the budgetary costs. Although the extent of consumer transfers is debatable, the studies quoted and the present discussion all agree that such costs greatly exceed the budgetary costs of the CAP. Clearly the sums involved in consumer transfers to producers are difficult to estimate whilst the budgetary costs are known exactly. This is one reason for the general neglect of consumer costs; a second may be the belief of bureaucrats and politicians that 'what the eye doesn't see the heart doesn't grieve over'.

Resource misallocation

Resources should be used so that they give the highest possible returns; any deviation from this ideal is misallocation. The CAP misallocates resources in three ways: first within agriculture, second between agriculture and industry, third between the EEC and third countries.

Within agriculture efficient producers should be able to expand at the expense of those who are less efficient; only by such productivity improvements will agriculture make the best use of its resources. Of course this is an economic judgement, which implies that some producers would enjoy higher incomes whilst others would be forced to accept lower incomes or to leave agriculture. The CAP was intended to raise the incomes of producers; in so far as it enables the inefficient to survive it also prevents the expansion of the efficient. This effect is particularly important between member states, which the CAP allows to distort competitive forces, notably through MCAs and by neglecting the existence of national aids. The income of society as a whole is reduced if one sector is less efficient than it might be.

Artificially raising agricultural prices far above their free market levels whilst manufacturing industries have to compete with other countries with but little protection, results in another form of resource misallocation. Resources used in agriculture are paid higher returns than they would otherwise obtain; they are therefore retained in agriculture instead of transferring to other industries. In terms of the earlier chapters, this resource misallocation can be represented as constraining the natural course of economic development during which resources are transferred from agriculture to other uses. When the Community's economies were prospering prior to the present recession, this argument was certainly valid. In the early 1980s there are no positive alternative uses for most agricultural resources and many would judge it better for resources to be inefficiently employed in agriculture than to be unemployed outside agriculture.

Misallocation between the EEC and third countries refers to the fact that many agricultural commodities could be imported at prices much lower than those ruling in the Community. Sugar is a case in point. Several countries could profitably sell sugar to the EEC at prices lower than those ruling under the CAP. They are not only prevented from doing so, but are also harmed by EEC sales of subsidized sugar in world markets. If the EEC were to reduce its level of protection and import from countries able to produce food more cheaply, those countries would enjoy higher incomes. They would then be able to buy more of the Community's industrial exports .... The progress of this argument is obvious, and so is its corollary, that the protective nature of the CAP reduces the total income of societies beyond as well as within the EEC.

Conclusion

The CAP system of administered prices has resulted in ever-growing surpluses and escalating disposal costs. Although large, these are not the major item of costs, being far exceeded by the costs to consumers who have to pay food prices much above those ruling in world markets. A further cost is the loss of other forms of production which resources devoted to agriculture might otherwise have produced – at least during the full employment years of the sixties and early seventies. The costs of the CAP are borne not only by the EEC but are also imposed through trade restrictions on other countries. So surpluses are the visible indication of massive costs, the bulk of which are unseen and therefore ignored (except by economists), but which are nevertheless real and important.

6 Common financing

This chapter considers the background to common financing and its position as one of the three principles of the CAP. Moving to the consequences of common financing, we examine in detail the international transfers which it causes. The implications for surpluses are then explored. Finally the damaging disputes between member states to which the present system gives rise are discussed.

Financing the CAP

The fundamental agreements establishing the CAP support system and FEOGA were reached during the 'stopped clock' negotiating marathon of 31 December 1961 to 14 January 1962. Deriving from this session is Regulation 25 on the financing of the CAP. This looks forward to the time when common prices will be achieved as a result of a Community-wide policy and states that 'the financial consequences thereof shall devolve upon the Community'. It continues by saying that the Fund will accordingly finance refunds on exports and market intervention (see Appendix 6.1).

The principle of common financing of the CAP thus introduced by Regulation 25 has become of fundamental importance. In a 1979 brochure explaining the CAP the Commission says that the three principles of *the single market*, *Community preference* and *financial solidarity* 'have become the golden rule of the CAP' (ECC 1979a, 12). Virtually every Commission document relating to the CAP reaffirms the essential nature and inviolability of these three principles.

The single market means common prices, which, as Chapter 4 demonstrated, have not existed since 1969: the single market has become a myth, a pretence permitted through the medium of MCAs.

Community preference is inherent in the nature of a customs union, which essentially consists of a group of countries which have abolished trade barriers between them in favour of common trade barriers around them against the rest of the world. This element of the Community is of course applicable to all sectors, not just agriculture. Clearly the consequence of Community preference is that member states trade with each other in preference to third countries. The variable levies on agricultural imports are calculated so as to have this effect. On industrial products the common external tariff is, with few exceptions, less than 10 per cent; for agricultural commodities the variable levies are on average equivalent to a tariff of the order of 100 per cent. So whilst the principle of community preference is the same for agriculture as for other sectors, the degree of preference is very different.

The remainder of this chapter is addressed to the third principle, financial solidarity, under which the Community budget is financed by the 'own resources' system and pays for the implementation of common policies – largely the CAP. The principle is regarded as the practical expression of the supranational nature of the Community. It thus has considerable political appeal for the federalists, not least many of the civil servants of whom the Commission is composed, who as idealists desire European integration above all else. It should be underlined that financial solidarity is a political, not an economic, concept. Had it been economically essential it would have been enshrined in the Treaty of Rome along with the other basic essentials instead of being left to secondary legislation some five years after the Treaty had been written. In other words there is no economic reason why the CAP cannot be financed directly through national exchequers instead of via a central fund. This argument will be returned to in Chapter 8. We now turn to the major consequence of common financing, the intercountry economic transfers to which it gives rise.

International transfers

In the previous chapter it was noted that the CAP transferred income from consumers to farmers. It follows that member states with a larger share of consumers than farmers transfer income to countries with a larger share of farmers – that is, net food importing countries transfer income to net food exporters. These transfers occur via the Community budget and through trade. It might appear that only the Community budget is relevant to the principle of financial solidarity, but, as will be explained below, the principle also has important effects on trade transfers.

Table 6.1, giving the details of each member state's contributions to and receipts from the Community budget, shows how the budget transferred income between countries in 1979. It can be seen that the main elements determining a country's gross contribution to the budget are its collection of agricultural levies and customs duties on imports, and the size of its economy as reflected in its VAT yield. As FEOGA is the major source of budgetary expenditure it is not surprising that member states' receipts are dominated by FEOGA. The net contributions column shows that in 1979 Germany and the UK transferred large sums abroad, benefiting mainly the agricultural exporting countries – the Netherlands, Ireland and Denmark. It is interesting to compare the net contributions with GNPs: in these terms the UK had the highest negative ratio, contributing over ½ per cent of GNP – that is, about the order of magnitude of the economic benefit to be expected from joining a customs union – whilst at the other extreme Ireland's GNP was augmented by almost 9 per cent. A redistribution of income from the UK to Ireland, a poorer country in terms of income per head, may be regarded as desirable but this argument certainly cannot be used to justify the transfer of income to the other major beneficiaries, one of which, Denmark, enjoys the highest income per head in the Community (see Table 6.4). One other column of Table 6.1 requires some explanation – that headed 'Financial compensation'. This arises because the UK's contribution was excessive in terms of the Dublin agreement and was therefore reduced by the amount shown. In turn, this necessitated increases in the contributions of other members. Without this adjustment the UK would have been by far the largest net contributor to the budget instead of being a close second – that is, the budget would have been redistributing income from the poor to the rich to an even greater extent.

Having shown the magnitude of budgetary transfers for one year we now need to examine the data for other years. Table 6.2 gives the net contributions for recent years, the calculations being on the same basis as for the previous table. Italy is seen to be a net contributor to the budget in most years although she is one of the poorest members in terms of income per head. The remainder of the table shows that the comments already made in relation to 1979 are applicable to the other years. In conclusion, the budget transfers income between countries on

Table 6.1 Budgetary contributions and receipts, 1979

million ECU

	Contributions 'own resources'						Receipts					Net contributions
	Customs duties	Agricultural levies	Sugar levies	VAT	Financial compensation	Total	FEOGA	Social fund	Regional fund	Collection costs	Total	
Germany	1586.6	263.7	146.3	2245.6	+165.1	4407.2	2592.1	61.4	46.0	197.5	2897.0	1510.2
France	754.2	96.5	152.3	1720.4	+163.0	2886.5	2549.4	93.7	103.6	98.9	2845.6	40.9
Italy	497.7	410.6	45.9	747.7	+91.9	1793.2	1341.3	156.3	143.7	96.2	1829.7	−36.5
Netherlands	485.6	313.2	37.8	453.6	+53.9	1344.1	1559.5	11.1	8.6	84.9	1664.1	−320.0
Belgium	335.7	229.7	30.9	329.6	+40.7	966.5	806.5	7.8	3.1	58.8	876.2	90.3
Luxembourg	3.8	0.1	—	14.9	+0.6	19.4	14.2	0.3	0.3	0.4	15.2	4.2
UK	1344.6	353.2	26.1	1302.6	−512.9	2513.5	589.7	201.9	165.7	168.6	1140.9	1372.6
Ireland	57.1	3.6	4.6	41.6	−2.2	104.6	602.1	38.8	32.9	6.3	746.2	−641.6
Denmark	124.3	8.0	21.1	183.2	—	337.4	783.2	24.5	9.1	14.9	831.7	−494.3
Total	5189.1	1678.6	464.9	7039.8	—	14 372.4	10837.9	595.7	513.1	726.6	12 846.6	1525.8*

Sources: Derived from Statistical Office of the EC (1982)

Notes: FEOGA receipts are on the basis that MCAs benefit exporters; 10 per cent of customs duties and agricultural levies are regarded as collection costs and are refunded

*The excess of contributions over receipts for the Nine reflects administration costs, overseas aid, etc

Table 6.2 Net contributions* to the EEC budget

	million ECU					
	1976	1977	1978	1979	1980	1981
Germany	1054	1467	597	1430	1909	2025
France	− 58	310	371	78	− 144	− 389
Italy	− 248	− 294	334	− 534	− 646	− 688
Netherlands	− 222	− 88	− 41	− 288	− 376	− 141
Belgium/Luxembourg	− 346	− 329	− 337	− 610	− 426	− 528
UK	90	− 126	228	849	609	730
Ireland	− 155	− 212	− 326	− 545	− 630	− 579
Denmark	− 294	− 293	− 381	− 380	− 295	− 263
Greece						− 167

Sources: Statistical Office of the EC (1982); *Agra Europe*, various
Note: *Net contributions after rebates to the UK MCAs benefit importers

a substantial scale but not on an equitable basis; indeed, in some cases it involves transfers from the poor to the rich! Because the receipts from the budget are dominated by FEOGA, it is the agricultural exporting countries which benefit most.

Returning to the basis of the CAP and the transfer of income from consumers to producers, consider the position of a food-importing country. If an agricultural commodity is imported from a country outside the Community the variable levy collected is paid into the Community budget, whilst a member state exporting an agricultural commodity to the world market receives an export refund; such transactions give rise to the budgetary transfers which have just been examined. But suppose the importing country had imported its food directly from the food exporting member, no variable levy is collected because the commodity is already priced at its high CAP level. Nevertheless an income transfer is involved, because the importer pays the CAP price which is equivalent to the world price plus the variable levy, whilst the exporter receives the equivalent of the world price plus export subsidy. The income transfer in this case occurs directly, from the consumers of one country to the producers of another. Such a transfer is termed a trade transfer. These transfers would occur without common financing, but the latter increases their size. This is because some food-exporting countries would not have such high agricultural prices if they had to finance the export subsidies for their surpluses themselves.

Whilst budgetary transfers are easily observed because the actual monetary sums are known and recorded, trade transfers have to be calculated. There are numerous ways of calculating trade transfers, so the results are necessarily subject to argument. One set of calculations was made for 1977–9 by Rollo and Warwick (1979) on the basis that common financing and Community preference were dropped and that the CAP continued to operate otherwise unchanged. In other words the CAP price levels and price policy instruments were operated on a national rather than a Community basis. Hence production, consumption and trade flows would be unchanged, but each country would operate its own FEOGA, collecting levies on imports and paying subsidies on exports. Such a situation may or may not be realistic; the crucial point is that it captures the consequences of common financing and Community preference in isolation from any other change. The results of this study are given in Table 6.3. Budgetary and trade transfers are both shown, the sum of these two items being the financial flows across the frontiers of member states caused by the present CAP and its financial arrangements. Two further points must be made about this table. First, the results were extended to 1979 with unchanged methodology for the House of Lords Select Committee on the European Communities (1981, p. xi). Second, the budgetary transfers shown are confined to transfers via FEOGA; since contributions are for the budget in general rather than specific sections of it, this requires the assumption that FEOGA's expenditure is funded in proportion to each country's share of the ratio of total budgetary contributions.

The trade transfers and budgetary transfers (FEOGA) shown in Table 6.3 are almost always in the same direction, as one would expect. It can be seen that in the last three years of the 1970s the CAP was paid for by the United Kingdom, Italy, Germany, Belgium and Luxembourg in that order, and benefited the Netherlands, France, Denmark and Ireland. The real significance of these income transfers is more clearly seen by relating them to income per head. Thus Table 6.4 shows that the poorest Community member, Ireland, gains most in relative terms but the next two poorest members, Italy and the UK, lost, whilst three members enjoying much higher incomes – one the highest in the Community – gain. With one major exception, the redistributive effects of the CAP are clearly perverse. If the EEC had been intended to redistribute incomes it would surely have aimed towards a more even distribution, not the reinforcing of existing inequalities.

Table 6.3 Estimated financial flows between member states arising from CAP

£ million

	1977			1978			1979		
	FEOGA transfers	Trade transfers	Total	FEOGA transfers	Trade transfers	Total	FEOGA transfers	Trade transfers	Total
Germany	−469	−355	−824	−122	−434	−556	−465	−125	−590
France	+126	+463	+589	+41	+575	+616	+255	+600	+855
Italy	−74	−488	−562	−344	−588	−932	+4	−700	−696
Netherlands	+255	+545	+800	+241	+605	+846	+329	+325	+654
Belg./Lux.	−12	−12	−24	+33	−54	−21	+49	−300	−251
UK	−470	−167	−637	−673	−110	−783	−882	−225	−1107
Ireland	+234	+168	+402	+343	+184	+527	+339	+275	+614
Denmark	+334	+209	+543	+408	+275	+683	+336	+375	+710

Source: Rollo and Warwick (1979)

Table 6.4   Gains and losses due to the CAP relative to income per head, 1979, and food self-sufficiency ratios, 1980

	GNP per caput EEC 9 = 100	Percentage change in GNP due to CAP	Self-sufficiency ratio 1980
Germany	134.9	−0.17	96
France	115.8	0.32	126
Italy	61.6	−0.46	83
Netherlands	115.2	0.93	216
Belg./Lux.	120.0	−0.47	130
UK	77.7	−0.59	86
Ireland	47.6	8.80	307
Denmark	140.2	2.27	237

Sources and notes: Second column is derived from the final colum of Table 6.3 and GNPs at market prices; the latter and column 1 are from Statistical Office of the EC (1982); self-sufficiency ratios are from Buckwell *et al.* (1982, 78)

Other studies of the redistributive effects of the CAP have been undertaken; Blancus (1978) covered the period 1970–6, Koester (1978) 1971–5 and Morris (1980) 1978. Their methods differ, and naturally their results differ to some extent, but their conclusions are broadly similar to those of Rollo and Warwick detailed above. There can be no doubt that the CAP has not only a major but a largely inequitable impact upon the economies of several Community members. Common financing also has indirect but very important effects on the surplus situation.

Common financing and surpluses

If one country operated a high price policy like the CAP, it would have to pay for the disposal of surpluses generated. Consequently its government would weigh carefully the benefits of higher prices to its farmers against the costs to its consumers and taxpayers of providing export subsidies. For some countries, the CAP's system of common financing divorces the benefits of high prices for producers from their financial consequences to consumers and taxpayers. As the cost of supporting milk production dominates FEOGA it may be used to illustrate the point. Koester (1978, 11) estimated the consequences of increasing the CAP price of butter by 1 per cent in 1974 to be an additional transfer of 6.8 million UA from the UK. Italy would also have made a small loss, but all the other Community members would have gained because they all produced butter surpluses. Under such circumstances it is hardly surprising if a majority of the Community argue in favour of higher milk prices; they are able to support their case with the fact that dairy farming is the major activity of the small farmers whose incomes are too low. It is likely that the intransigence of the milk surplus problem owes something to the fact that the burden of financing the surplus is only partly borne by those who produce it.

Common financing not only encourages some countries to favour higher CAP prices, it also encourages them to use national subsidies in order further to expand their agricultural industries. Indeed, the present system persuades *all* member countries that agricultural expansion is desirable. Taking the UK as an example, if food production could be expanded until no imports were necessary, the country's contributions to the Community would be reduced because there would be no agricultural trade transfers and budgetary transfers would no longer include levies on agricultural imports. Agricultural exporting members wish to produce and export more food because their income gains via the budgetary and trade transfers are thereby augmented. Of course, for both food importers and exporters, agricultural expansion means that Community surpluses rise and so do disposal costs. In essence, each country hopes that its expansion will reduce its CAP losses or increase its CAP gains more than its share of the additional costs of extra surplus disposal. It is a sad paradox that in the present context the interests of the Community as a whole are diametrically opposite to the self-interest of its individual members.

Disputes over financial arrangements

In earlier chapters attention was drawn to the frequent fierce arguments over financing the CAP. The 'own resources' system was supposed to have ended these difficulties by replacing national contributions, which had to be negotiated every year, by an automatic system whereby duties and levies plus a share of VAT receipts accrued to the Community. Unfortunately the advantage of circumventing acrimonious annual negotiations was flawed because the new system had no equitable basis. On the contributions side the extent of a country's liability depended substantially upon whether or not it was a major importer; its receipts similarly depended on the extent to which it exported food. In the original Community of Six, Italy was consistently a net contributor to the Community despite being the poorest member whilst two richer members, France and the Netherlands, were the only countries to be net beneficiaries.

Since the 1973 enlargement of the Community, the UK has become a major loser due to the budgetary arrangements, despite being one of the poorer members in terms of income per head. In 1977 and 1978 the UK was the major net contributor to the Community budget even after her contributions had been 'corrected' according to the mechanisms agreed during the renegotiation of her terms of accession. In 1979 her net contribution, after 'correction', just fell short of Germany's. UK dissatisfaction with this situation was made very plain by Mrs Thatcher following the election of a new Conservative government in 1979. She demanded, publicly as well as privately and somewhat stridently, a revision of the budgetary arrangements. Before and during the 1980 price-fixing negotiations the UK made it clear that no prices agreement for the 1980/1 marketing year would be reached until budgetary arrangements more favourable to the UK had been concluded.

Eventually the Council of Foreign Ministers, in yet another marathon meeting on 29 and 30 May, adopted a three-year formula to reduce the UK's contributions to the budget. The formula is complex (see Appendix 6.1) but certainly offered the prospect of major reductions in the UK's net contributions up to and including 1982. An important part of the agreement was that the Commission should, by the end of June 1981, come forward with proposals to resolve the problem by means of structural changes in Community budgeting. This charge for the Commission became known as the 30 May 1980 Mandate (ECC 1980d). Superficially it appeared to promise a fresh look at the whole area, but its terms of reference said that the proposals for change should be made 'without calling into question the own resources system of raising revenue or the basic principles of the CAP'. The stated aim was to prevent unacceptable situations for any member country. Evidently little room for manoeuvre was provided. As the Mandate is concerned with reform, it and the price reviews of 1981 and later – which might be expected to be influenced by its reform proposals – are discussed in Chapter 8 along with other aspects of CAP reform.

Conclusions

Common financing has been shown to be an arbitrary method of financing the budget in general and the CAP in particular. It involves major intercountry financial transfers via the Community budget. These are often inequitable, with two of the three countries having the lowest *per capita* incomes contributing substantial sums for the benefit of richer countries. If the Community had been intended originally to redistribute income between countries, which it was not, it would surely have chosen a fairer method of doing so, involving economic convergence rather than divergence. It may be that the inequitable aspects of the system were not foreseen when it was designed. Now that they have become obvious it seems perverse of the Commission to continually emphasize the sanctity of 'the three principles' and of the own resources system.

The inequitable income redistributive effect of the budget has been seen to be reinforced by trade transfers. These are difficult to estimate so that the results are debatable; but lack of precision does not diminish their significance; they should be an overt part of CAP and budgetary arguments but tend to be ignored.

Finally, common financing is particularly perverse because it divorces decision from financial responsibility. It encourages *all* members to expand agriculture in order to maximize their net receipts or minimize their net contributions, even though the Community as a whole has a serious agricultural surplus problem.

Appendix 6.1 Temporary solution to the budget problem, 1980-2

At its marathon meeting of 29–30 May 1980 the Council of Foreign Ministers adopted a three-year formula to reduce the UK's net contribution to the Community budget. The formula is complex but is basically an adaptation of the Dublin financial mechanism agreed in 1975 (detailed in Chapter 3).

Essentially, the Commission estimates the net contributions which the UK would make in the absence of corrections. These are then reduced by 66 per cent, giving agreed rebates which should be credited to the UK in the budget of the following year. Alternatively, if the UK so requests, the Council of Ministers may, on a proposal from the Commission, make advance payments.

The agreement reached in 1980 includes the following calculations for the years 1980 and 1981:

UK net contributions to budget, million ECU

	1980	1981
Commission estimate	1784	2140
Agreed rebate (66 per cent)	1175	1410
Adjusted net contribution	609	730

The possibility of the UK contributions exceeding the Commission estimates was allowed for as follows. In 1980, if the UK contribution exceeded 1784 million ECU, the extra would be born as to 25 per cent by the UK and the remaining 75 per cent by the other eight members. In 1981, if the UK's net contribution after adjustment exceeded 730 million ECU, the first extra 20 million ECU would be borne wholly by the UK; from 750 to 850 million ECU, 50 per cent would be borne by the UK; and above 850 million ECU, 25 per cent would be borne by the UK. In each case the remaining percentages would be shared out among the other eight members.

Regarding 1982, the Community was pledged to resolve the problem by means of strucutral changes in Community budgeting; the Commission was to submit proposals by the end of June 1981 (this is the 30 May 1980 Mandate discussed at length in Chapter 8). If this was not achieved the arrangements for 1980–1 were to apply.

REGULATION NO. 25
on the financing of the common agricultural policy

Republished in *Secondary Legislation of the European Communities*, vol. 14, London, HMSO, 1973.

TITLE 1

Single market stage

Article 2

1   Revenue from levies on imports from third countries shall accrue to the Community and shall be used for Community expenditure so that the budget resources of the Community comprise those revenues together with all other revenues decided in accordance with the rules of the Treaty and the contributions of Member States under Article 200 of the Treaty. The Council

shall, at the appropriate time, initiate the procedure laid down in Article 201 of the Treaty in order to implement the above-mentioned provisions.

2   Since at the single market stage price systems will be standardised and agricultural policy will be on a Community basis, the financial consequences thereof shall devolve upon the Community.

The Fund shall accordingly finance:

(a) refunds on exports to third countries;

(b) intervention aimed at stablising markets;

(c) common measures adopted in order to attain the objectives set out in Article 39 (1) (a) of the Treaty, including the structural modifications required for the proper working of the common market, provided that those measures do not encroach upon the work of the European Investment Bank and the European Social Fund.

7 Achievements of the Common Agricultural Policy

The success of any policy must be judged in relation to its objectives. This chapter considers the CAP firstly in terms of the achievement of the specific objectives laid down for agriculture in Article 39 of the Treaty of Rome. It then proceeds to examine the CAP in the light of Article 110 and in terms of the general economic rationale of the Treaty. State aids to agriculture, *un*common items distorting a supposedly common policy, are also examined. A concluding section summarizes the chapter's findings and outlines the major elements of the dissatisfaction which give rise to demands for reform.

Appraisal of the CAP in terms of Article 39

In the previous chapter the 30 May 1980 Mandate was noted, under which the Commission was required to produce reform proposals by the end of June 1981. In December 1980, as a first step towards fulfilling this Mandate, the Commission published *Reflections on the Common Agricultural Policy* (ECC 1980a) which gave the Commission's view of the CAP and laid down guidelines for the future. The present appraisal draws extensively upon this document. Where changes over long periods are important the data in this section relate to the original Six because they are the only members to have enjoyed the CAP over an appropriate length of time. The objectives are discussed in the order in which they appear in Article 39.

INCREASED PRODUCTIVITY

One aspect of productivity, yields, has been examined in Chapter 5, where it was shown that major increases in output had occurred. Indeed these increases have been embarrassingly large, resulting in considerable surpluses. The Commission estimates the annual rate of increase in output to be 2.5 per cent (ECC 1980a, 4) and comments 'we can see that the CAP has encouraged the modernization of European agriculture.' This assertion does not necessarily follow from the fact that production has increased, for two reasons. First, similar increases in output have occurred in virtually all developed countries since the Second World War, notably in the USA and in the UK prior to accession to the Community, when both countries operated policies very different from the CAP. It would be more reasonable to attribute these increases to the application of scientific progress – which is independent of the CAP. Second, it might be argued that because the CAP has raised prices above their free market levels the survival of many small inefficient farms has been permitted, thereby *retarding* the modernization of European agriculture.

Following the Commission's line in *Reflections* the discussion has been in terms of output, but the relevant part of Article 39 refers not to production but to *productivity* (production per unit of input), emphasizing the particular importance of labour productivity. Clearly, with major increases in output and massive declines in agricultural employment there have been substantial increases in labour productivity. Table 7.1 shows that productivity increased more rapidly in the first five years of the 'completed' CAP (1968–73) than in the following five years – the result of a much smaller outflow of labour in

Table 7.1 Labour productivity in the Six

	Annual percentage change in labour productivity in agriculture		Ratio of output per worker in agriculture and in total economy (%)	
	1968-73	1973-78	1968	1979
Germany	7.9	4.1	44	34
France	7.1	2.3	48	54
Italy	4.9	3.5	47	50
Netherlands	6.9	5.0	87	68
Belgium	8.5	2.8	88	84
Luxembourg	5.9	3.0	46	44
The Six	6.3	3.4	54	52

Source: Derived from ECC (1980b), 158, 168-9

the latter period as recession reduced non-agricultural employment opportunities. Despite its substantial growth of labour productivity, agriculture's performance has not matched that of the remainder of the economy. The final two columns of Table 7.1 show that output per worker in agriculture compared very unfavourably with the output per worker for the total economy in both 1968 and 1979, with a slight tendency towards a worsening of the situation over this period.

It must be concluded that agriculture's improved labour productivity still leaves it trailing very badly behind the remainder of the economy and consequently that the CAP is a failure in this respect.

A FAIR STANDARD OF LIVING FOR THE AGRICULTURAL POPULATION

This section of Article 39 carries on 'in particular by increasing the individual earnings of persons engaged in agriculture'. The level to which earnings should be increased before they could be regarded as fair is not stated. In recent years agricultural incomes have been compared with average non-agricultural incomes on a regional basis; the Commission's usage of this comparison has endorsed it as the appropriate criterion of 'fairness'.

In *Reflections* (ECC 1980a, 5) the Commission says 'since 1968 real income in agriculture has on average increased by 2.8% a year, a rate equal to the increase in other branches of the economy over the period 1968-76'. This bland statement implies that all is well, 'the CAP has enabled agricultural incomes to keep on growing ... it has protected the sector from the recessions' (ibid.). All is *not* well, and the use of percentages in this manner is grossly misleading; indeed the impression given is that deception is intended, for in the 1960s agricultural incomes in the Six were approximately half those enjoyed in the non-agricultural sector, so if both increase at the same percentage rate the *absolute* difference will *increase*. The Commission's statement has also been described as misleading by the UK's National Farmers' Unions, both because the measure of income used is 'inadequate' (it ignores wages, interest, rent and depreciation) and because it 'fails to draw attention to the very serious decline in farm incomes registered in some EEC countries since 1976 and in all countries since 1979' (House of Lords Select Committee 1981, 60; evidence given by Comité des Organisations professionnelles agricoles de la CEE). The NFUs attempt to put the record straight by giving their own data, but naturally select data which display to their own advantage the decline in farm incomes of which they complain – their data relate to aggregate income whereas it is income per head which is important. In Table 7.2 these data have been more fairly re-expressed in these latter terms; they still support the farmers' complaints, showing that incomes have declined since 1976 and, further, that by 1980 there had been very little improvement from the inadequate income levels of 1968.

Many structural and income data in agriculture are difficult to interpret because they are in terms of the total number of farms and the total number of farmers, though in reality many farmers are part-time or hobby farmers whose main source of income is in the non-agricultural sector. In the Nine, 64 per cent of farms were part-time in 1980 (ECC 1980a, 11). Table 7.3 is restricted to 'market-oriented' farms, those where the farmer's income is primarily agricultural, and compares such incomes with the average in the non-agricultural sector on a regional basis. The disparity between agricultural and non-agricultural incomes varies considerably between countries. Only in the UK are incomes in the two sectors reasonably comparable; at the other extreme over 80 per cent of German and Luxembourg farmers have low incomes compared to the average for their regions; for the Nine the corresponding figure is 64 per cent. These data confirm the earlier findings of this section, that on average farm incomes are low.

Table 7.2 Index of net farm income per person in real terms

	1976 = 100						
	1968	1976	1977	1978	1979	1980	1981
Germany	88.4	100	94.4	92.8	74.3	64.5	62.4
France	75.6	100	99.0	101.0	107.8	84.5	78.8
Italy	87.7	100	99.9	105.3	110.3	95.6	89.0
Netherlands	84.4	100	90.7	91.6	81.7	90.3	105.8
Belgium	67.8	100	79.2	85.8	76.5	71.5	82.6
UK	73.0	100	86.6	78.0	64.4	48.2	48.4
Ireland	70.4	100	127.7	132.1	91.5	59.3	59.5
Denmark	97.9	100	121.2	116.7	66.1	63.0	73.0

Sources: Derived from net farm incomes in real terms in House of Lords Select Committee (1981), and employment data in Statistical Office of the EC (1982) and ECC (1981c, 1982a)

Table 7.3 Percentage of market-oriented farms attaining certain levels of income per person, 1977–8

Level of agricultural income	Percentage of holdings									
	Germany	France	Italy	Netherlands	Belgium	Luxembourg	UK	Ireland	Denmark	The Nine
Less than 80% of the non-agricultural income for the region	82	67	63	46	54	82	32	52	70	64
Between 80% and 120% of the non-agricultural income for the region	13	20	17	22	25	15	20	21	21	18
More than 120% of the non-agricultural income for the region	5	13	20	32	21	3	48	27	9	18

Source: ECC (1981c)

There is considerable income disparity within agriculture, even within one state, between regions, and between farms of different sizes and types. Regional disparities are greatest in France and Italy; in the former the extremes in 1978 were Ile de France and Limousin, farmers in the latter having incomes only one-sixth of those of farmers in the former. In Italy in 1978 incomes in Lombardia were three times those of Molise. The smallest disparities existed (in 1977/8) within Germany, where incomes in Schleswig-Holstein were 40 per cent higher than in Hessen, and in the UK where the East Anglians received incomes 50 per cent higher than the farmers of Northern Ireland. The Commission has expressed its disquiet over these disparities and noted that they have increased as a result of the CAP. Thus 'the common market organisations tend to favour the more well-to-do producers, who are mainly concentrated in the richer regions' (ECC 1980a, 8) and 'the regions with the highest agricultural incomes are those which incur the most expenditure [i.e. FEOGA expenditure]' (p. 13). A brief consideration of the system will explain why the CAP benefits the rich farmers rather than the poor (although the latter provide the justification for income support). The CAP raises prices, it therefore raises revenues in proportion to output, so the largest farmers receive the most benefit. They also have the lowest average costs because of the importance of economies of size in agriculture.

Providing a fair standard of living for the agricultural population is the fundamental objective of the CAP. Using the Commission's concept of what constitutes a 'fair' standard it is clear that the CAP has not only failed *on average* to achieve this objective, but it has also *increased the disparities* within agriculture, enriching the rich rather than the poor. It should be noted that there is a major conflict between the objective of greater equity in terms of incomes and the general economic rationale of the Community. This topic will be explored later in the chapter.

MARKET STABILITY

The objective of stable prices has certainly been achieved. The CAP's interventionist system has resulted in less price variation than in world markets or in those of the USA. Indeed the variable levy method of price support used for the main products isolates Community prices from the influence of external changes, whilst the intervention and export subsidy aspects remove the price consequences of internal changes (i.e. surpluses) also. Stability is desirable because it enables farmers to plan and hence invest efficiently. However, too much stability prevents the price mechanism carrying out its allocative functions. For example temporary gluts cannot be disposed of through price reduction. In essence, the administered prices which are responsible for stability prevent consumer requirements, especially in terms of quantity, being transmitted to producers, and are thus one dimension of the surplus problem. Hence the achievement of price stability is a mixed blessing.

ASSURANCE OF REGULAR SUPPLIES

Surpluses have been discussed at length in Chapter 5; self-sufficiency ratios for all major food stuffs were shown to have increased along with the concomitant costs of surplus disposal. It might be argued that surplus disposal costs are preferable to food shortages. The Commission makes this intrinsically appealing point thus:

> We need only think of the dependence of Europe as regards energy and of the vulnerability of supplies from overseas in order to understand that an entity such as Europe, with a population of 260 and perhaps soon more than 300 millions, cannot afford to rely on others for its food supplies and has the duty to exploit the richness of its soil. (ECC 1980a, 5)

How vulnerable would overseas supplies be? The suppliers would be predominantly those in the 'new world', of European extraction, with European-type cultures, political systems and sympathies, such as the USA, Canada, New Zealand, Australia, etc. Clearly, it is nonsense to suggest that these suppliers are likely to form themselves into a price cartel which the energy analogy implies. There is of course a second aspect of vulnerability – the possibility that overseas supplies might be curtailed in the event of military conflict; certainly the heavy dependence of the UK on imported foodstuffs proved to be extremely inconvenient in two world wars (although at the outbreak of the First World War when the UK imported half its food no serious hardships were involved in coping with severely reduced supplies – at least no one starved). Two questions may be posed: is the possible war to be nuclear or 'conventional' and, if the latter, what level of dependence on overseas supplies might be construed as being vulnerable? If the war was to be nuclear, food supplies would be irrelevant; if conventional then a considerable reduction in the present self-sufficiency ratios could occur without causing concern. Indeed the Commission's preoccupation in recent years has been how to reduce output, as will be seen in the following chapter. There is no doubt that despite its statement quoted above, the Commission would be very pleased if regular supplies were somewhat less assured than they have been during the lifetime of the CAP.

REASONABLE PRICES TO CONSUMERS

What is reasonable in this context is nowhere defined. *Reflections* has no specific comment relating to this objective; consumer interests, as is usual in Community agricultural contexts, are virtually ignored. As the definition of reasonable is a matter of opinion there is little scope for analysis here, but it must be noted that because of the protective nature of the CAP, food prices have been substantially higher than in world markets. Because low-income consumers spend a higher proportion of their incomes on food than other consumers they are particularly disadvantaged by the CAP. As the CAP benefits the rich rather than poor farmers there is an element of transferring income from poor consumers to rich farmers. This is surely not an intended or desirable feature of the CAP.

ACHIEVEMENT OF ARTICLE 39 OBJECTIVES: CONCLUSIONS

The Commission's *Reflections* begins by stating that 'the CAP has broadly achieved its main aims' (ECC 1980a, 26). This amazing conclusion is reached because the *Reflections* document is not so much a rigorous analysis of the situation as a threadbare justification. Taking the Article 39 objectives in order: it is true that productivity has increased, but as argued above, this is largely due to factors beyond CAP; fair incomes, using the Commission's definition of fairness, have not been achieved, indeed the relative position of farmers appears to have deteriorated since 1968; stable prices and assured supplies have certainly been achieved, but it is difficult to describe food prices as reasonable for consumers. Above all, the fundamental objective of the CAP is to raise farm incomes to a 'fair' level; this it has signally failed to do.

Appraisal of the CAP in terms of Article 110

This Article has as its first paragraph:

> By establishing a Customs Union between themselves the Member States intend to contribute, in conformity with the common interest, to the harmonious development of world trade, the progressive abolition of restrictions on international exchanges and the lowering of customs barriers.

It is evident that the CAP is entirely incompatible with these good intentions. Community preference, expressed through large variable import levies, has progressively closed Community markets to the agricultural products of more efficient foreign suppliers. At the same time, by the growth of subsidized agricultural exports the Community has also taken their traditional markets from these third countries. It is not surprising that the Community's activities are a source of distress and anger to other agricultural exporting countries. The Australian Government has set out the effect upon Australia in a memorandum submitted in evidence to the House of Lords Select Committee on the European Communities as follows: 'Prior to the CAP, Australia secured and held European markets (mainly, but not of course solely, Great Britain) for its farm products on the basis of price and quality considerations' (House of Lords Select Committee 1982a, 127). The memorandum continues to explain how the CAP resulted in the loss of Australia's markets for farm products in the EEC, illustrated by Table 7.4.

A concluding paragraph says that:

> The reality of virtual exclusion from the Community market, the growth of subsidised exports, and the resulting disruption of international markets and prices, is at the root of Australia's concerns. The CAP is working in ways that are fundamentally contrary to the open trading system embodied in the General Agreement on Tariffs and Trade (GATT) and the objectives of the Treaty of Rome. (ibid., 130)

New Zealand has been badly affected by the CAP because over 70 per cent of her export earnings came from farm products. The New Zealand view of the CAP is that

> First, it places severe limits on New Zealand's ability to export the temperate agricultural products which it produces most efficiently

Table 7.4 EEC (9) share of Australian exports

	per cent		
	1958-9	1965-6	1979-80
Beef and veal	71	31	2
Dairy products and eggs	69	58	0
Sugar	48	47	0
Wheat	48	12	0

to its natural (and traditional) markets in Europe; secondly, it impedes New Zealand's efforts to develop satisfactory alternative markets, through the subsidised export of the Community's own relatively inefficiently produced surpluses of the same products. (ibid., 157)

The harmonious development of world trade is clearly not encouraged by the CAP, yet the Community is the world's largest trading entity and its industrial exports depend heavily upon an open world trading system. There is thus a major conflict between the objective of a liberal trade policy (implied by Article 110) which operates for industrial products, and the agricultural trade policy which is one of the most protective in the world. These conflicts could at any time involve more than logic: they could erupt into damaging trade wars. The House of Lords Select Committee evidently envisaged such possibilities when it stated that

it must be questioned whether it is in the Community's wider interests to continue to pursue its present agricultural trade policies or whether it should take account of their possible repercussions. For it must be remembered that the Community is dependent on many of the third countries concerned – developing and developed – both for raw material supplies and for markets for its industrial exports. (ibid., para. 62, p. xxvi)

Appraisal of the CAP in terms of the Treaty of Rome

The economic rationale of a customs union is that production and trade are allowed to occur freely within the customs union area and so be determined by comparative advantage. That is, each country specializes in the production of the goods which it can produce most efficiently, trading these with other countries' goods which it can only produce less efficiently; such exchanges benefit all participating countries. This specialization means that efficient firms and industries expand, but they can only do so if less efficient firms and industries contract: the process involves the transfer of resources from the inefficient to the efficient. The economic rationale behind common agricultural prices and free intra-Community trade is thus that farm products should be produced in the regions to which they are most suited. Inevitably, in each region the less efficient farmers would be forced out of business. This economic logic, as Marsh has expressed it in evidence to the Select Committee, 'is elaborately defied by the CAP, which establishes administered prices which attempt to prevent market forces forcing vulnerable farmers to leave the industry' (House of Lords Select Committee 1981, 34).

The particular mechanisms by which the CAP prevents change are, first, the high price system, which enables many inefficient farmers to survive who would otherwise be forced to leave; and, second, the system of green exchange rates and MCAs which distorts competition between countries. The price consequences of these were examined in Chapter 4; now consider the effect in relation to the prevention of change. Wheat provides a suitable example: high prices in Germany since the 1969 revaluation have encouraged German farmers to produce more wheat than they would have at the lower prices ruling in France. At lower prices the less efficient German wheat producers would have reduced output, but consumption would have increased, providing the more efficient French producers with a better market. In their turn the French have managed to prevent the adoption of a competitive sheepmeat regime because it would have ruined many thousands of French lamb producers. An almost endless list of examples of such changes prevented by the CAP, against all economic logic, could be compiled.

In *Reflections* (ECC 1980a, 3) the Commission shows that common financing is another important factor in distorting competition via high prices and MCAs because the financial consequences of increased output do not fall directly upon the country producing the excess. The Commission is in fact attempting to show that 'single prices' would not have been agreed without common financing but the argument illustrates the former point quite adequately. Thus: 'Would Ireland accept high prices for beef and veal if it had to bear the consequences from its own budget?' and 'Would France have agreed to high prices for cereals and sugar for 15 years if it had had to meet the expenditure itself?' and again, 'Would Italy have subsidised olive oil or processed fruit and vegetables to the same extent if the Italian Parliament had had to vote the necessary appropriations each year?' The Commission continues: 'The answer is clearly no.'

State aids

The CAP was supposed to enable the more efficient agricultural producers to expand and improve their share of the Community market. In practice, with the exception of Italy, all members have increased their self-sufficiency, so that intra-Community agricultural trade has offered reduced rather than enhanced opportunities to exporting countries. France in particular, despite her relative efficiency in a number of products, has seen her share of the Community market fall considerably. In exasperation the agricultural exporting member states have attempted to increase their shares by using national aids, often regardless of their legality. In summer 1980 the Commission listed 51 illegal aids being used by member states, 39 of these being in France (Pearce 1981, 48). Repeated requests from the Commission to explain or remove these aids have been ignored despite the Commission's declared intention of taking these cases to the European Court. Remarkably little is known about state aids for agriculture. The House of Lords Select Committee (1982b, para. 43) have complained that 'It has been public knowledge for some time that the Commission had prepared an inventory of state aid to agriculture; but much mystery surrounds the document.' Although the Commission has kept the details hidden, it does mention state aids briefly in its annual report on *The Agricultural Situation in the Community*: recent issues (up to 1981) give the total expenditures on state aids as being about double those of FEOGA.

Four recent cases of national aids which have been alleged to significantly distort competition may be used to illustrate the problem.

Common prices for the 1980–1 marketing year were agreed late after protracted negotiations. The French Government decided to compensate its beef and dairy farmers for the consequent loss of two months' price increases and spent some 400 million francs (about £44 million) in so doing. The Commission took this matter to the Court, but no formal decision was reached. Later in 1980 the French Government announced an aid package of 4.1 billion francs. The Commission ruled in July 1981 that much of this aid was incompatible with the Treaty of Rome and should be abolished. Not only was this finding ignored but the new French government announced in December 1981 an additional aid package amounting to 5.6 billion francs!

Netherlands horticulturalists have, since the major oil price rises of the early 1970s, enjoyed a preferential tariff for heating fuel. After several years' consideration the Commission was unable to declare this to be an illegal state aid because the state owned only 50 per cent of the fuel company involved, and instead authorized other member states to grant temporary aids to their own producers.

Finally, there is the controversy over the apparently massive support given by the French government to a turkey processing plant in Brittany. The multiplicity of aids from different sources provided for this plant render the exact scale of assistance impossible to calculate. What is known is that in the summer of 1981 French processors were offering turkey in the UK at 39–41 pence per pound, which is estimated by the Ministry of Agriculture to be below production costs (House of Lords Select Committee 1982b, 125–6). The Ministry also noted that the plant's annual production of 100,000 tonnes of turkeymeat was approaching the total UK production. It seemed likely that this plant would rapidly put all UK producers out of business, but in the event they were saved by a change in UK poultry health regulations which completely stopped turkey imports from France. In turn, exports of British lamb to France have been severely disrupted by their being intensively tested for the presence of growth hormones which are in fact not used in the UK.

In addition to the huge quantities of state aid which the Commission admits are provided there is considerable assistance in some member states in the form of undertaxation. Only the UK, the Netherlands and Denmark oblige all of their farmers to present accounts for taxation purposes. In the other countries the majority of farmers are assessed on a purely notional basis. The French Tax Council estimated that in 1979 French farmers were undertaxed to the extent of 3200 million francs. This is equivalent to a subsidy of the order of £10 per hectare. Similar calculations in Germany suggest a subsidy of about £30 per hectare! (House of Lords Select Committee 1982b, evidence given by K. P. Riley, p. 47).

Two facts emerge from this discussion. First, vast and partly covert national aids are used to benefit farmers. Second, these measures are not harmonized: on the contrary, they are *ad hoc* and designed to serve specific regional and national interests. Common prices may be a necessary condition for a common policy but they are not a sufficient condition. Even the Commission acknowledges that the present extent of national aids is a serious distortion of competition.

Conclusions

The agricultural problem to which the CAP is primarily addressed is that of relatively low incomes. As discussed in the first chapter, there is a chronic tendency for agricultural incomes to be low as the natural consequence of economic development. Low earnings are the result of productivity in agriculture increasing more rapidly than the demand for food, and result in cheaper food and the transfer of labour to more highly paid activities, though this transfer is slow; agriculture is slow to adjust to economic change. The slowness of adjustment leaves agriculture with an excess of labour, and an uneconomic farm size structure – that is farms are generally small and therefore high cost.

It is essential to see the CAP in the context of agriculture's role in economic development. In aiming to raise farm incomes to approximate those in the non-agricultural sector the CAP is attempting to reverse the tide of development. It is of course failing to do so. To change the metaphor, the CAP treats the symptoms of the disease but leaves its causes untouched or even exacerbated. The plain truth is that if supply outpaces demand prices must fall to restore the balance; as aggregate agricultural income falls, average incomes can only be maintained if labour leaves at a sufficiently high rate. These facts were well recognized in the Mansholt Plan of 1968, which stated that price support alone could not achieve the objectives of policy; it proposed the modernization of agriculture involving a greatly accelerated reduction in the number of farmers. By preventing prices restoring equilibrium the CAP has prolonged the existence of small uneconomic farms and generated expensive surpluses.

The failure of the CAP is comprehensive. It has totally failed to improve the relative position of the agricultural population even on average. Within this it has benefited the rich farmers and regions rather than the poor, largely at the expense of consumers, the poor bearing the major burden because they are both more numerous and spend a higher proportion of income on food. Major transfers of income between countries, caused by common financing, have also to a considerable extent been inequitable. Harsh economic effects have been imposed on third countries, generating ill-will and the potential seeds of destructive trade wars. The national incomes of the Community countries have been reduced by an unknown but significant extent. The CAP has even failed to be a *common* policy and has added to rather than reduced distortions to competition within the Community.

The reader may well wonder why this chapter has as its title the *achievements* of the CAP. It might be justified on the grounds that achievements may be negative, but there is one sense in which the CAP is a remarkable positive achievement. It is a monument to the determination of politicians to work together for a united Community. Because the CAP is the first major common policy involved in the integration process it has become the symbol of co-operation. In this spirit of determined co-operation the politicians have nurtured the CAP in defiance of economic logic and the long-term interests of the Community.

8 Reform of the Common Agricultural Policy

This chapter begins with a brief review of the major faults of the CAP as a background to its reform. It has been observed that the CAP suffers two types of surpluses – one of commodities, the other of reform proposals. A complete account of such proposals would certainly occupy more space than is available here, and the present text is accordingly restricted to reviewing critically the major categories of reform. Then the events and debates of the early 1980s are described and analysed because they have been particularly concerned with reform and clearly illuminate current thinking. Finally the author has the temerity to add his own ideas to the existing surplus of reform proposals.

Faults in the CAP

Despite the description 'common', the policy has one common feature only – that of financing, for MCAs and green currencies have maintained very *un*common price levels. 'Fair' incomes for the agricultural population are the primary objective, but this has not been achieved on average and the distribution of incomes within agriculture is particularly wide. Resources are misallocated within member states, between member states, and between the Community and the rest of the world. In this last instance, the CAP's large-scale dumping of surpluses on world markets is a threat to the free world's trading system as a whole. The distribution of the costs of the CAP is inequitable, involving income transfers from poor consumers to rich farmers and from poor countries to rich countries.

The visible symptoms of this catalogue of illnesses are the high and disparate prices of agricultural commodities, the surpluses which they generate and the high budgetary costs of their disposal. Proposed reforms range from superficial treatments of these symptoms to radical measures intended to promote a cure. Only one minor proposed reform is not controversial: this is gradually to abolish MCAs to restore the common prices element of the CAP. The other proposals frequently made will now be considered in turn.

Reform proposals

CHANGES IN RELATIVE PRICES

In the 1960s the Community was self-sufficient in relatively few products. To reduce or remove existing surplus problems it was proposed that the prices of commodities in surplus should be reduced relative to other commodities. The Community was then a major importer of beef, and a 'conversion premium' was introduced to persuade dairy farmers to switch from milk production – already the major surplus product – to beef. Changed relative prices could have reinforced such a switch. A relative reduction in the price of cereals was canvassed because this would have reduced output and at the same time expanded the use of cereals for animal feeding stuffs. The respectability of these proposals was emphasized when in 1973 a group of distinguished agricultural economists embraced them in the *Wageningen Memorandum* (See Swann 1978, 187). Increasing self-sufficiency in almost all major products has since that time made such proposals obsolete. Even when changed relative prices constituted a fashionable proposal the motive was merely to reduce FEOGA expenditures on surplus disposals without tackling any of the CAP's other blemishes.

PRODUCTION QUOTAS

The discussion of this topic is prefaced by a description of the only quota system currently applied in the Community – the case of sugar beet. Extracting sugar from beet requires large capital-intensive factories whose capacity must be fully utilized if costs are to be minimized. To achieve this processors conclude contracts with producers and purchase only such contracted supplies. A producer's contract is clearly equivalent to a quota. Individual quotas of this type restrict competition because there is no price competition – factories buy at fixed prices and so have no incentive to purchase from the most efficient producers. Thus the latter's opportunities to expand are constrained whilst the less efficient are shielded from competition.

Sugar beet factory outputs are limited by national quotas. In each factory region a 'basic quota' defines the output of beet to which the full intervention price applies; for production beyond this level up to a 'maximum quota' the intervention price is subject to a 30 per cent levy. Additional output receives no official support. (Sugar levies accrue to the Budget and hence help to defray the costs of surplus disposal.) Global quotas of this nature limit financial support but increase uncertainty: they make future prices a matter of guesswork, making it difficult for farmers to plan output efficiently. This point is even more obvious in proposals to extend global quotas to other commodities: intervention prices would be limited to a Community-level quota, excess output being sold at world prices, and farmers would receive a weighted average of these two prices. Intervention prices would, as now, be known in advance, but farmers would have no means of knowing either the total Community output nor the future world price of the commodity, and hence would be planning output without knowing the price which they would eventually receive.

Summarizing, individual quotas restrict competition and hence reduce production efficiency, global quotas increase price uncertainty and so also reduce efficiency. However, quotas may be used either to limit surplus production or the costs of disposal. They have no other attractive features, but individual farm quotas are necessary in the special case of sugar beet to ensure the constant supply of beet required to keep down processing costs.

CO-RESPONSIBILITY LEVIES

The principle of co-responsibility is that the financial consequences of surpluses should be shared between the Community and the producers, instead of being borne entirely by the Community. If farmers produce too much they should have to help to dispose of surpluses. The implication that farmers are, at least in part, responsible for surpluses is not very logical. A surplus is an excess of production over consumption. Since prices determine both output and consumption the cause of surpluses is clearly intervention in the price mechanism. High prices expand output but reduce consumption; high prices are set by the Community. From a different angle, an individual farmer plans output according to market prices; his output is too small to influence market prices. It is unreasonable to set high prices and then blame him for responding logically to them.

Co-responsibility levies have been applied to milk since 1977. Rates of levy have to date been very low, reaching a peak of 2.5 per cent in 1982. Attempts to raise the levies to levels which would be effective have proved unacceptable to the Council of Ministers. To become effective levies would have to be high enough to help to finance surplus disposal and they would concomitantly reduce output and income. There have been attempts to discriminate between different sizes of producers, with small producers paying lower or no levies. This may be equitable between producers on income grounds, but would also discriminate against efficiency since the larger producers are also more efficient; UK objections to such size discrimination reflect the fact that British dairy herds are on average much the largest in the Community.

In reality co-responsibility levies are no more than covert price reductions. Being covert and justified on plausible (although illogical) grounds makes them apparently more politically acceptable than direct price reductions. Their apparent acceptability rests on the premise that farmers do not regard them as price reductions. The ineffectual rate of the milk co-responsibility levy suggests that decision-makers have little faith in this argument.

CONSUMER SUBSIDIES

The sale of Community surpluses to other countries at greatly reduced prices has been widely criticized. Large quantities of butter exported to Russia at prices far below those ruling in the Community's member states are a particular cause of anger. Sales of such surpluses in Community markets would only be possible at greatly reduced prices; if farmers' prices were not to be similarly reduced the differences would have to be met as subsidies. Conventionally these have been termed consumer subsidies although they should more properly be called farmer subsidies, since consumers would enjoy lower prices initially if it were not for the existence of price supports.

There are some minor subsidies already, notably for butter all the year round in the UK and briefly at Christmas in other member states. 'Consumer' subsidies big enough to sell all Community surpluses within the common market would cost far more in budgetary terms than the present support system, assuming farm prices to remain at current levels. They are therefore unlikely to become more widely used. Such subsidies have one major advantage over the present system: the main burden of CAP costs would be shifted from consumers to taxpayers – that is, the cost burden would be shared out in proportion to ability to pay rather than according to food needs.

REDUCED SUPPORT PRICES

Josling and Marsh have both proposed policies which would involve significant price reductions and which are therefore far more radical than the reforms so far considered. Josling (1973, 95–8) has suggested that prices should be reduced at least far enough to remove surpluses, but recognizes that even efficient producers would then suffer low incomes. They would be compensated for low prices by price supplements (this system is similar to the deficiency payments method of price support used in the UK before accession to the EEC), sufficient to give them reasonable incomes. Inefficient farmers – those with small farms or farms in disadvantaged areas – would need additional support before their incomes could be regarded as reasonable. Josling proposed that these farmers should be given income supplements, that is payments related to need rather than output, but that such payments should be limited either in duration or to the current generation of farmers. Josling's scheme has much to recommend it. Lower prices would not only remove the budgetary costs of surplus disposal but also result in better resource allocation within the Community and between the Community and the rest of the world. Consumers would benefit from lower prices and support costs would be borne more equitably by taxpayers. Finally, whilst inefficient farmers would not be penalized for being trapped in agriculture, the limitation on income supplements would persuade the next generation to enter some other sphere. The ultimate success of such a scheme would thus be a more modern agriculture. There are, however, important social costs: the eventual removal of inefficient farmers – the vast majority of farmers – and hence the destruction of rural communities over large areas.

Marsh's proposals are based on the replacement of common prices by a system of common *trading* prices which would offer a margin of protection perhaps similar to that for industrial products (Marsh 1977). Member states would be free to maintain prices for their own farmers at whatever level they chose but would have to trade with other members at the common trading prices level. Thus an exporting country would have to tax or subsidize its exports to bring them to the common level, and imports would similarly have their prices lowered or raised to the internal price level by subsidies or taxes. It is instructive to consider the proposals in relation to surpluses. The Community, as at present, would finance the dumping of surpluses on the world market and the costs would be lower than at present because the common trading price would be nearer to the world price. But the countries producing the surpluses would have already had to subsidize them down to the common trading price level. Thus the main financial consequences of surplus production would fall upon the countries producing them. This would possibly moderate the extent of surplus output.

The abandonment of common internal prices which Marsh's proposals involve is a matter for criticism. Common food prices are essential if competition is not to be distorted. However, as noted earlier, common prices are a necessary but not sufficient condition for free competition: other conditions are also necessary, for example common taxation, but this is not yet contemplated. It could also be argued that the disparate price consequences of Marsh's proposals are no worse that the actual price differences already existing and tolerated because of MCAs. The proposals have two major merits, both resulting from the major costs of surplus disposal falling upon the governments of the surplus producers: first, surpluses would be discouraged, presumably by lower prices which would improve resource allocation and the lot of consumers; second, the present inequitable transfers, both budgetary and non-budgetary, between member states would be greatly reduced. Broadly, the proposals involve the continued existence of a common policy, which is politically necessary, and allow member states to support their farmers to any extent which *they themselves* are willing to finance.

RESTRUCTURING

Proposals to alter the structure of agriculture are based on the premise that small farms are inefficient and generate low incomes. The available evidence supports this premise. Small farms are inefficient in the sense that they have high production costs compared to large farms because of the existence of economies of size (colloquially termed economies of scale) in agriculture. Because small farms produce small quantities of output their revenues are small; low revenues and high costs lead necessarily to low incomes. Restructuring implies a reduction in the number of small farms, so that those remaining on the same total land area will be larger and hence more efficient. Such changes are in line with the forces of economic development.

The Mansholt Plan of 1968 contained radical suggestions by which the Commission proposed to modernize agriculture, ending up with large efficient farms able to generate fair incomes for farmers. A concomitant reduction in the number of farmers was clearly necessary and led to Mansholt being dubbed 'the peasant killer'. As noted earlier, the hostility with which this Plan was received embarrassed the Council of Ministers into ignoring it. At the time the Plan was published the EEC was experiencing rapid growth. In the late 1970s, as the recession began, opportunities for the re-employment of farmers in the non-agricultural sector rapidly declined. Mansholt, then retired, stated his opinion that small farmers were better off farming, albeit inefficiently, than becoming unemployed (Mansholt 1979). In the early 1980s, with the numbers of unemployed exceeding the numbers of farmers, few would dissent from Mansholt's opinion.

The Guidance Policy does contain some restructuring elements introduced before the recession, as noted in Appendix 3.2 summarizing the CAP. Their impact has so far been negligible, but the analysis of restructuring should be continued on the grounds that booms tend to follow recessions.

Is restructuring desirable? On economic grounds the discussion so far suggests that it is, subject to the availability of off-farm employment. However, a case could be made on social and environmental grounds for the retention of at least the bulk of the existing farmers. This topic is explored later in this chapter; for the present, the conventional viewpoint that the 'modernization' of agriculture is desirable will be adopted. Then what are the economic consequences of restructuring? The answer has to be related to the conditions under which it occurs. The argument is that restructuring will modernize agriculture which will then no longer need income support – but in the meantime income support is necessary. This is extremely naive because it completely ignores the existence of time. Restructuring takes time: to modernize Community agriculture would take many years. During this process income support in the form of high prices is generally assumed to continue, in which case the investments in buildings and machinery associated with modernization would be at levels appropriate to high prices. A removal of price support would render such investments unprofitable, and would therefore be impossible or at best incomplete. It follows that restructuring would optimally occur within a lower-price framework. In the interim, compensation for low prices would be necessary; a form of direct income support would be required. An examination of this topic follows anon.

The assumption that a restructuring policy would occur against the background of the current type of high-price policy is implied by the Mansholt Plan's recognition that one consequence would be extra output. This is because large farms adopt new techniques more rapidly than small farms and so increase productivity. The Plan suggested that to compensate for extra output resulting from modernization it would be necessary to reduce the area of land utilized by agriculture. Land retirement was also seen as a consequence of structural reform by the Vedel Report on French Agriculture (Ministry of Agriculture, Paris 1969). Any such retirement does not fit in well with a desire for structural reform because a reduction in the area of land must raise its price – assuming the demand for land to remain constant. Since the demand for land is derived from the price of its products the importance of the product price situation is again emphasized. Any rise in land prices increases the capital required to amalgamate small farms into large ones and thus limits the ability of farmers and landowners to restructure their holdings.

DIRECT INCOME PAYMENTS

These are payments made to people for being farmers. They could be related to need, with most or all expenditure concentrated on small farmers; prices could then be reduced to lower levels with all the attendant benefits which have been discussed above. It is generally proposed to limit direct income payments either to the present generation of farmers or to a fixed period – say twenty years. Small farmers would then not be replaced by their heirs; as they departed, their vacated land would be added to neighbouring farms. Thus, agriculture would gradually change from predominantly small inefficient farms to large efficient ones. This transition would have occurred without disadvantaging the existing generation of farmers.

Direct income payments have become the conventional route recommended by economists for reaching an agricultural utopia – or at least giving farmers fair incomes without causing surpluses. Remarkably, there is little analysis into this area. Their attraction for economists is that direct income payments would not, unlike prices, be related to output. This brings two benefits: first, prices would be freed from their income-supporting role and returned to their original role of balancing supply and demand; second, raising incomes via direct payments would not automatically cause output to increase. Indeed, according to the logic of economic analysis, output would be determined solely by prices and costs, and entirely independently of direct income payments. No one knows whether farmers are as logical as economists or if they would in practice use extra income to invest in their farms and so raise output. The author's personal experience of farmers leads him to suspect that many would obtain the same enjoyment from new farm buildings or tractors as other people would from extending their houses or buying new cars – that is, they would invest their increased incomes in their farms.

Whether or not direct income payments would have a significant impact on output, they would shift the burden of support from consumers to taxpayers and through concomitant price reductions bring about an improvement in resource allocation. Both consequences are economically desirable.

The 30 May 1980 Mandate

In the spring of 1980, agreeing agricultural prices for the 1980/1 harvest year proved, as usual, to be extremely difficult. The UK government, elected the previous summer, was determined to reduce the UK's net budgetary contribution, which they alleged to be unfairly large. To facilitate this the UK made it clear that only a happy budgetary outcome would permit a prices agreement to be reached. The temporary budget arrangements (for 1980 and 1981) which resulted were discussed above in Chapter 6 and detailed in Appendix 6.1. It was agreed that a more permanent solution to this budgetary problem was required and the Commission was mandated to propose such a solution in the following terms:

> For 1982, the Community is pledged to resolve the problem by means of structural changes (Commission mandate, to be fulfilled by the end of June 1981: the examination will concern the development of Community policies, without calling into question the common financial responsibility for these policies which are financed from the Community's own resources, or the basic principles of the CAP.

Taking account of the situations and interests of all Member States, this examination will aim to prevent the recurrence of unacceptable situations for any of them). If this is not achieved, the Commission will make proposals along the lines of the 1980 to 1981 solution and the Council will act accordingly. (EEC 1980d)

Subsequently the Commission published three documents in response to the Mandate. The first, *Reflections on the Common Agricultural Policy* (EEC 1980a), has been extensively referred to in Chapter 7; the second, coming at the end of June 1981, was the *Report on the Mandate* (EEC 1981b). The third, published in April 1982, was *A New Impetus for the Common Policies*; it deals with all the common policies and includes a section 'Guidelines for European Agriculture' (EEC 1982b) which is an expansion of some of the points made in the *Report on the Mandate*. These publications will be discussed as displaying the current views of the Commission on the need for changing the CAP and the nature of the reforms which they propose. The 1981 and 1982 price reviews will be examined as evidence of the political response to these proposals.

Throughout the three documents, the 'three principles' (discussed in Chapter 6 above) are emphasized as given. The *Mandate*, as noted above, has written into it that the examination of Community policies is to take place 'without calling into question the common financial responsibility for these policies'. *Reflections* is at pains to show that financial solidarity is essential because otherwise some countries would not have agreed to high common prices (discussed in Chapter 7), but manages to ignore the corollary that financial irresponsibility is thereby encouraged. The important point is that there is no new thinking here, and radical reforms such as those of Marsh, analysed above, are immediately ruled out.

Reflections begins by examining the CAP in relation to its objectives, concluding that they have been broadly achieved. As Chapter 7 showed, such a conclusion is somewhat generous and not universally shared. The *Report on the Mandate* and 'Guidelines' assume without further discussion that the objectives have been achieved, thus: 'the objectives of the Treaty of Rome – be it security of food supplies, satisfaction of consumers' requirements, increased productivity or higher farm incomes – have been achieved' (EEC 1981b, 11). Despite this 'achievement' there is a recognition that not all is well. *Reflections* rather defensively examines a number of common criticisms of the

CAP, rejecting many but admitting to two major problems – surpluses and that the main beneficiaries of the CAP are the richer farmers and regions rather than the poor. The *Report* is also partially defensive, beginning its diagnosis of problems with 'it is neither possible nor desirable to jettison the mechanisms of the CAP but on the other hand adjustments are both possible and necessary' (EEC 1981b, 11). The surplus problem is then described: 'technological progress and the play of market organisations mean that the Community is now more than self-sufficient for most major products' (ibid.). The Commission's attitude illustrated by these quotations is that the CAP is basically satisfactory and only requires adaptation; radical reforms are certainly not to be entertained.

Having decided that surpluses are the major problem the *Report* says that 'the imperatives of sound market management, combined with budgetary constraints, therefore call for improved control of the unwelcome effects of the operation of market organisations' (EEC 1981b, 11). There follow some conclusions which represent a significant change from traditional attitudes. Previously intervention or 'guaranteed minimum' prices were applied to any quantity of production (except for sugar, limited by quota, and milk's minor co-responsibility levy). Now, the Commission asserts that prices should be fixed with regard to wider considerations than farm incomes alone, these considerations being the degree of self-sufficiency, consumers' interests and 'market realities'. Of particular importance is the statement that 'it is neither economically sensible nor financially possible to give producers a full guarantee for products in structural surplus' (p. 12). The Commission also seems to be more conscious of financial constraints than in the past. Thus the *Report* states in its preamble that 'there can be no development of Community activities as long as the Community budget remains artifically limited by the current ceiling on its resources. It will take the initiatives required to have this constraint removed' (EEC 1981b, 7–8). Later it says that if its proposals are implemented the result will be 'that agricultural spending in the years ahead will grow less rapidly than the Community's own resources' (EEC 1981b, 13). An unusual shaft of light is indicated by the statement that the proposed solutions 'should be combined to achieve the objectives set by the Treaty at as low a cost as possible' (EEC 1981b, 12). This suggestion that the CAP should achieve its objectives *efficiently* in terms of cost is unique, and certainly overdue.

The solution to the CAP's problems are set out in *Reflections* and expanded by the other two documents. They relate to three areas: the adjustment of market organizations, a new approach to export policy, and the adaptation of structural policy. Before analysing them it is interesting to note the background, outlined in 'Guidelines', against which the solutions must be implemented. It is remarked that in the Community there are 9 million unemployed and that agriculture employs 8 million; and the Commission predicts that the rate of economic growth in the period 1980–5 will be perhaps half that of 1973–80 – itself low (EEC 1982b, 66). By noting these facts the Commission is making it clear that the time is not ripe for modernizing agriculture with a concomitant massive reduction in agricultural employment. A more subtle swipe at the intensive methods which have exacerbated surpluses must delight the environmentalists:

> the adaptations should take into account the impact of agriculture on the environment and the need to preserve the natural resources that form the basis of agricultural activity, and to ensure the preservation of wild life and natural habitats (EEC 1982b, 68).

This recognition that agriculture involves much more than food production is to be welcomed, though a cynic might observe that the wildlife and habitats to be preserved appear to be small farmers in their small farms!

ADJUSTMENT OF MARKET ORGANIZATIONS

This rather opaque phrase means that guaranteed prices should no longer be high and open-ended. The *Report* proposes three elements of price policy. First that the gap between Community prices and those of competitors 'in a better organised world market' (EEC 1981b, 12) should be narrowed; second that prices should be designed to improve the balance of production; and the third proposal is for the 'modulation of guarantees in line with Community production targets' (ibid.). Narrowing the gap between Community and world prices would reduce both the output of surpluses and the export subsidies required to dump them on world markets. Lower cereal prices in particular would reduce production costs of certain livestock products and hence lead to a better 'balance of production'. Of prime importance is the phrase 'modulation of guarantees in line with production targets', the full implications of which are spelt out in

'Guidelines'. Cereals may be taken as the example. In 1981 the Council agreed in principle to reduce cereal intervention prices in 1982/3 if output exceeded 'basic quantities' (EEC 1982b, 76). The Commission proposes to define such a basic quantity, now termed a 'production objective', as EEC consumption plus current exports, and to limit intervention to such a quantity. Similarly for milk, extra output would result in a supplementary levy on dairies sufficient to pay for the disposal of increases in production over consumption. Naturally, the details differ between products but the general principle is to set production targets and apply price penalties for exceeding them. This is clearly a proposal set within the concept of co-responsibility which, as remarked earlier, is believed to be more acceptable politically than overt price reductions.

Supplementary to the adjusted price policy are proposals to improve quality control and to tighten financial control of FEOGA expenditure. In essence the first proposal would result in less produce being accepted for intervention which would in itself reduce surpluses. Tightening financial control of FEOGA expenditure is a reference to the fact that some governments regularly manage to be over-generous with FEOGA monies. France heads the list here by overspending usually to the tune of 10 per cent. Finally, the Commission realizes that price reductions at Community level could be neutralized by some member states expanding national aids. Therefore 'Guidelines' promises that the Commission 'will use its right to refuse FEOGA cover for expenditure by a Member State under the common market organisation if this Member State has paid a national aid in contravention of a market organisation' (EEC 1982b, 74).

NEW APPROACH TO EXPORT POLICY

This is first applied to imports with the Commission desiring to curb the import of cereal substitutes used for animal feeds. Because of international trade agreements, which render them subject to little or no import duty, these substitutes are cheaper than cereals and so have been imported in growing quantities, thus increasing the size of the cereals surplus.

In the price policy proposals above, it was noted that the gap between Community and competitors' prices *in a better organized world market* should be narrowed. The Commission signifies by this italicized phrase an intention to raise world prices by agreement with other major exporters. Since the demand for food imports from world markets is certain to be diminished by such price rises, this implies a reduction in total supplies. The consequences of such price increases on poorer countries who are net food importers – many of them developing countries – are ignored. However, returning to the implied reduction in supplies one may wonder what reduction would be necessary for the Community. Apparently none: 'the objective of Community export policy should be to increase its agricultural exports so as to at least maintain its share' (EEC 1982b, 69). How to achieve an agreement to give the Community higher export prices *and* at least the same volume of exports is a subject not explored. 'Guidelines' continues with its desire to expand exports by saying that 'to that end, the Community may prefer, or even be compelled, to use a wider range of mechanisms in the export field' (ibid.). One such mechanism is mentioned, the possible use of long-term contracts to supply agricultural products to non-member countries. To whom does the Commission envisage consigning agricultural exports in the 1980s? Its assessment is that 'the countries likely to become the Community's main customers are the East European countries (including the USSR), a number of developing countries and Japan' (ibid.). Apparently Russia buys butter cheaply from the Community to sell to Russian consumers at much higher prices, doubtless applying the profits to good causes! Exporting cheap food to Japan will doubtless help the Japanese to remain competitive and export their industrial goods to the Community! The Commission have yet to devise rational economic arguments to justify their export policy.

ADAPTATION OF STRUCTURAL POLICY

This third element of solutions follows naturally from the first element's proposed price reductions. Previously price support has been the vehicle for the social policy of raising farm incomes; if prices are to play a smaller part it is necessary to find some other way of raising incomes. Thus in *Reflections* (EEC 1980a, 13) the Commission states that the solutions must 'not be allowed to lead to a drop in living standards for those involved'. Structural proposals are to aid 'qualified' farmers to adapt to the changing situations, with further aid for those who cannot adapt or who live in areas where it is felt desirable to maintain a farming population. The *Report* (EEC 1981b, 12) refers to 'the possibility of income support policies to certain producers in specific circumstances' and to structural policies 'tailored to the needs of individual agricultural regions'.

THE SOLUTIONS - ARE THEY SOLUTIONS?

The proposed changes in price policy are sensible in that price reductions are involved, though straightforward price reductions would be more effective and efficient than co-responsibility measures. It also seems reasonable to compensate producers via appropriate structural policies, though the form which these might take is only vaguely indicated. Sadly, the proposed export policy seems ill-founded. The desire to narrow the gap between EEC and competitors' prices is to be satisfied partly by raising world prices, yet the Community wishes to maintain its agricultural exports. The Commission needs to take its own advice here and have regard to the 'realities of the market'.

THE SOLUTION TO THE BUDGETARY PROBLEM

In the face of all the Commission's criticisms, defences and proposals concerning the CAP, it is easy to lose sight of the fact that the Mandate was for the Commission to propose a permanent solution to the budgetary problem. The *Report* eventually does get round to some positive proposals. It identifies the Guarantee Section of FEOGA as the sole source of problems, stating that

> under present circumstances, the UK obtains a much smaller financial benefit from the CAP than the other Member States on account of the special features of its agriculture. Community solidarity demands that a remedy be found to this inequitable situation. (EEC 1981b, 16)

The remedy proposed is to compare 'the UK's share of Community GNP with the proportion it obtains of FEOGA guarantee expenditure' (ibid.) and to give a fairly high level of compensation for the shortfall. This should be financed from 'own resources', or if these are exhausted, by abatements on other countries' receipts. In the latter case the position of the less prosperous members (Greece, Ireland and Italy) should be protected. Finally, any compensation should be used to finance activities in the UK which accord with Community policies and with economic convergence in mind. The Commission suggests that its budgetary proposals are necessary because the implementation of its guidelines for reforming the CAP would not have a significant impact for some time.

It should be noted in passing that the proposed Mandate budgetary solution is not concerned with non-budgetary transfers. Though the latter are demonstrably very large they are ignored both by the Commission and by UK governments.

The 1981 and 1982 price reviews

Producers' incomes had fallen in 1980 so it was not surprising that for the 1981/2 year the Community's farmers should demand very large price increases averaging more than 15 per cent. The Commission, continuing to pursue what for several years it had termed a 'prudent' price policy, proposed increases averaging 7.8 per cent. In line with their emerging Mandate proposals they also proposed a super levy (of up to 30 per cent) for milk and the extension of the co-responsibility principle to other products. Whilst modest price increases and production curbs were welcome to the UK and Germany, these proposals were greeted in other member states with a sense of outrage; prolonged and difficult negotiations appeared certain. In March the lira was devalued by 6 per cent followed by a revaluation of sterling by 23 per cent. Since the ECU is defined as a weighted average of Community currencies its value showed a net increase, setting off a series of further devaluations – in France, Italy, Denmark, Ireland and Greece. By also devaluing their green currencies these countries automatically secured raised agricultural prices in terms of national currencies, and since it was this group of members which most wanted to raise Community farm product prices their pressure to this end was abated.

Towards the end of March the European Parliament called for a 12 per cent increase in prices and rejected most of the Commission's proposals for restraints. Most significantly they rejected the proposed milk levy and any additional co-responsibility levies. Eventually the Commission raised its price proposals to average 9.45 per cent and persisted with its co-responsibility intentions. Although the prices package was adopted by the Council of Ministers the only further restraint on output to be accepted was an increase in the existing milk levy from 2 to 2.5 per cent.

It will be remembered that the 30 May 1980 Mandate arose from the need to find a permanent solution to the UK's budgetary problems, but that an interim mechanism had been agreed to operate until the end of 1982. In the spring of 1982 these financial mechanisms had compensated the UK for her 'unfair' net contributions far more than had been anticipated. As shown in Table 8.1 the UK actually made a budgetary gain in 1981. It seemed likely that this unexpected event would complicate the 1982 price review negotiations. Indeed, negotiations were prolonged and heated, with the UK (conscious that the current budgetary compensation mechanism had been agreed only to the end of the year) refusing to reach a prices agreement before the future of the budget had been settled. Progress on the budget issue was nil. On the prices front the Commission had proposed an average increase of 9 per cent and as usual larger increases had been demanded by the farmers' organizations and several of the agriculture ministers. In the Council of Agriculture Ministers an average increase of 10.4 per cent was virtually settled, final agreement being refused only by Mr Walker, the UK minister. He made it clear that although he was in sympathy with this prices package and willing to accept it, he would not do so until the Council of Foreign Ministers had settled the Budget issue. This position was very inept: had he claimed that the budgetary consequences of such large price increases – which exceeded the rate of inflation – made the price increases *themselves* against the UK's national interest, he could legitimately have used the power of veto under the Luxembourg Compromise. But having admitted his acceptance of the price rises in principle he courted disaster. The other members of the Council took the proposed price increases one by one and agreed each by majority voting. The UK delegation was furious,

Table 8.1   UK net contributions to the Community budget, 1980, 1981

	million ECU	
	1980	1981
Deficit estimated by Commission	1784	2140
Agreed UK rebate (66%)	1175	1410
Estimated net contribution	609	730
Actual UK deficit	1507	1376
Actual UK payment	332	−34

Source: Agra Europe, various

the British press and Parliament outraged by this perfidious alleged breaking of the Luxembourg Compromise. Clearly the latter was not really broken because it was not involved, owing to the absurd negotiating stance adopted by the UK. So price increases averaging 10.4 per cent were 'agreed'; in terms of national currencies some minor green currency devaluations raised this average to over 12 per cent. No new measures to curb surplus production were introduced.

At the end of May 1982 the Council of Foreign Ministers agreed to give the UK a budgetary rebate under the existing temporary arrangements (see Appendix 6.1). A minimum rebate of 850 million ECU was agreed. The cost of this rebate should have been shared amongst the other members according to a budget key. Germany objected to paying a full share, having been the main contributor in the past, so it was agreed that Germany's contribution to the UK rebate would be half her 'normal' share, and the shares of the other members were therefore increased. Of course the net burdens of the budget, after these manipulations, still left the UK and Germany as the only net contributors. Implementation of this settlement for 1982 proved very difficult. In December the required supplementary budget was rejected by the European Parliament, partly in an attempt to extend its powers over spending but also as a protest over the way in which the 1981 rebate had been absorbed by the UK Exchequer instead of being used in Community-approved social or regional projects. In spring 1983 the 1982 rebate was eventually rescued by the Foreign Ministers, who also agreed in principle to the payment of a 1983 rebate, but it seemed likely that the latter would have strings attached specifying the manner in which it was to be used.

The Mandate is dead

In response to the 30 May 1980 instruction to propose a permanent solution to the UK's 'unacceptable' budget problem, the Commission produced a two-stage solution. In the long term they proposed reforms which were intended to reduce the costs of the CAP, so permitting the expansion or introduction of policies having more of an 'urban' content; these would have benefited the UK. In the short term, whilst these reforms took effect, they proposed temporary financial mechanisms to compensate the UK for her excessive net contributions to the budget. In the 1981 price review the Council of Ministers refused to introduce any of the surplus-reducing measures outlined in *Reflections* published six months earlier – except for raising the milk co-responsibility levy from 2 to 2.5 per cent. The *Report on the Mandate* itself and its supplementary 'Guidelines' were almost totally ignored in the 1982 price review settlement, and the only concession to the Commission's line made by the Council was the agreement to make rather trivial adjustments to the prices of cereals, colza and milk if output exceeded threshold levels in 1982 (see Appendix 8.1); the milk co-responsibility levy was reduced to 2 per cent. Hence the link between budget restructuring and the reform of the CAP, which was central to Commission thinking, was broken.

It is evident that the politicians have no real desire to reform the CAP. In the 1980s eight members benefit from the existing budgetary transfers; only Germany and the UK are net contributors, and such a minority is powerless to force change. In the face of the collapse of the Commission's reform proposals and the lack of a permanent solution to the UK's 'unacceptable' budget situation, the Mandate is obviously dead.

The budget–CAP reform link

In its Mandate documents the Commission proposed to reform the CAP in order to permit a restructuring of the budget. History suggests that this is putting the cart before the horse. Only when the budget appears likely to run out of funds can politicians be persuaded to give serious consideration to CAP reform. From the Community's point of view the budgetary problem is that there is a ceiling on revenue – 'own resources' – but not on expenditure. In the mid-1970s the rate of growth of expenditure – largely on the CAP – began to exceed the rate of growth of 'own resources'. At the end of the decade the Commission's 'prudent' agricultural price policy had reversed this situation but resulted in significant reductions in real farm incomes. Consequently pressure for price increases, resulting as noted above in large price increases in 1981 and 1982, mean that expenditure is now outpacing revenue. Relatively high world prices in these two years reduced the costs of surplus disposal, permitting CAP price increases without breaching the budget but leaving little scope for price increases in the future.

The 1983 price review

Farm incomes increased in 1982 by an estimated 5 per cent in real terms so the upward pressure on prices was less than in recent years.

The Commission's opening proposal was for a 'normal' price increase of 5.5 per cent. Normal in this context is what might be considered appropriate in the absence of significant output increases. In practice the thresholds set in 1982 for milk, cereals and colza were substantially exceeded, implying the operation of price penalties. Sugar and tomatoes were also singled out as requiring smaller price increases because of surplus problems.

Negotiations were, as usual, difficult and protracted, and so delayed the introduction of new price levels beyond the normal date for the beginning of a marketing year. In addition to the expected UK obstructiveness intended to facilitate the settlement of a budget rebate in her favour for 1983, there were various demands for green currency devaluations, and from the Italians – being close to an election – a request for special interest rate subsidies. It had earlier been agreed that green currency adjustments should await a price settlement, and despite some objections this position was not changed. However, in May the UK chose to agree to price increases without waiting for a budget settlement because a UK general election had just been announced and the proposed price increases, being smaller than in recent years, might be passed off as a government triumph. Giving way to the Italians' demands removed the last obstacle and a price settlement was reached on 17 May. In terms of ECUs the price increases averaged 4.2 per cent – just below the average rate of inflation. However, farmers are paid in national currencies, not ECUs, and after some subsequent green currency devaluations the average price rise in national currencies was 6.9 per cent. In conjunction with the continuing advance of yields this price settlement will not moderate the growth of surpluses nor the costs of their disposal. Indeed, as noted in Chapter 9, under existing arrangements the budget's 'own resources' are virtually certain to be insufficient to meet rapidly rising costs by the end of 1984. The detailed application of the price penalties agreed in 1982 and introduced in 1983 are given in Appendix 8.1. They show that despite stated intentions, the Council of Agriculture Ministers is still unwilling or unable to reach price decisions which would significantly reduce surpluses.

Rethinking the problem of reform

It seems essential, to this author, to rethink problems from first principles. The basic problem is that incomes in agriculture are judged to be too low, necessitating government intervention to raise them to a 'fair' level. As discussed in Chapter 1, in the course of economic development agricultural productivity increases, and the extra output can only be sold at lower prices so that relative resource returns (especially for labour) are reduced, and labour is thus persuaded to leave agriculture for other sectors where incomes are higher. *The desire to raise agricultural incomes is social policy and can only be achieved by the distortion of economic forces.* This distinction between social and economic forces and the conflict between them is fundamental. One important conclusion follows immediately: if the income problem is due to an excess of labour in agriculture, achieving the social objective of 'fair' incomes will ensure that the excess labour will stay where it is. There is therefore no solution to the agricultural income problem; it is with us for ever, either in the form of low incomes or excess labour, or (as at present) both simultaneously. The second conclusion follows logically: intervention in agriculture will always be necessary; in the interests of the well-being of society as a whole such support should be efficient, that is at least cost.

In searching for a least-cost method of implementing the social policy the present CAP presents a catalogue of pitfalls to be avoided. Thus its high prices result in resource misallocation, including serious trade distortion, impose heavy costs on consumers and taxpayers, and benefit the rich rather than the poor. In 'free enterprise' economies it is accepted that only the market can efficiently allocate resources. The inequitable income distribution which a free market generates is 'corrected' in our society by income transfers – the taxation of the rich and social payments (old age pensions, child benefits, unemployment benefits) to the poor. Agriculture should not be an exception. If agriculture was accorded the same level of protection as other sectors, resources would be allocated as efficiently as possible – given the excess of labour resources retained in the industry through raising incomes. The question is how should this income transfer be arranged? As for other sectors, the income should come from general taxation. How can it be applied to the poor but not the rich? A simple suggestion is to pay all *full-time* farmers (there is no reason to aid part-time or hobby farmers having other sources of income), perhaps defined as those obtaining at least three-quarters of their income from agriculture, a standard lump sum each year. To benefit, a farmer would be required to present full accounts each year; in addition to normal taxation a surcharge would be added to recoup aid progressively at higher incomes. At a certain income level the aid would be entirely recouped and the surcharge would cease to apply on additional income.

There are three major reasons why the above type of policy has never been implemented and is regarded as extremely unpalatable. First, farmers regard 'fair' prices (meaning high prices) as their right and social payments as demeaning charity. This is particularly true of the larger, richer farmers who, having the education and time to become leaders, plead the cause of the poorer farmers but realize that their own interests are best served by high prices. Second, politicians are aware of farmers as a large body of voters, numerous enough in many areas of the EEC to sway election results. Farmer prejudices must therefore be accommodated. Third, large numbers of politicians and not a few of the top layer of bureaucrats are themselves farm or estate owners, and consequently imbued with the rectitude of high prices. Of course no one would suggest that their self-interest is conscious, but unconscious self-deception is one of the few rational explanations of their irrational decisions.

Even obvious national and Community level benefits of an efficient agricultural policy may fail to appeal to politicians who have to 'sell' policies to voters. In the present instance one selling-point is that a lump-sum payment would reward small farmers for their contribution to the environment – large modern farms with their large fields and reduced hedgerows are, rightly or wrongly, disliked by the increasingly vociferous 'green' movement. However, whatever farmer votes such a policy might lose, they should be far outweighed by the votes gained from consumers enjoying lower food prices. Other benefits are that free markets do not produce chronic surpluses, and freed from these cares of the CAP, a rejuvenated Community would be able to concentrate on other areas; after all, the Community now has more people unemployed than in agriculture.

Appendix 8.1 Thresholds agreed in the 1982 price review to apply in 1983–4

Cereals. If average production in the three most recent years exceeds the set threshold level of 119.5 million tonnes, the intervention price for the following year is to be reduced – by 1 per cent for each 1 million tonne excess. Also, if imports of cereal substitutes exceed 15 million tonnes (which they have not yet) the extra is to be subtracted from the threshold.

In 1982 the harvest was estimated to be 124.5 million tonnes, giving a three-year average (1980, 1981, 1982) of 120.85 million tonnes and so exceeding the threshold by over a million tonnes. The price penalty imposed was a reduction in an increase which meant a net price rise of 3 per cent in ECUs for 1983/4. This is an increase of about 6.5 per cent in national currencies. Clearly this will not be an effective disincentive to cereal growers.

Rapeseed. Arrangements closely parallel those for cereals above. The threshold is 2.15 million tonnes, target and intervention prices to be reduced by 1 per cent for every extra 50 thousand tonnes. The threshold was exceeded in 1982 by approximately 50,000 tonnes so that price increases for the following year were reduced in the 1983 review. As the net increase was still 4 per cent in ECUs or 5.7 per cent in national currencies, the output is not likely to decline.

Milk. The threshold is the volume of milk delivered to dairies in 1981 (96.23 million tonnes) plus the estimated increase in Community consumption (0.5 per cent). Intervention prices are to be reduced by 1 per cent for every extra 1 per cent of milk delivered. The trend yield increase of recent years has averaged 1.5 per cent per year, and a continuation of this trend would thus cause small reductions in the support price but would increase the surplus by about 10 per cent per year!

In 1982 milk output rose by more than the trend suggested, the increase being 2.7 per cent. Consequently the Commission proposed a 2.2 per cent reduction in price. After allowing for this the target price agreed in 1983 still showed a net increase of 2.3 per cent in ECUs or 4.5 per cent in national currencies. The co-responsibility levy was unchanged at 2 per cent.

9 The Common Agricultural Policy: immutable or transitional?

Despite widespread criticisms and a plethora of reform proposals – some dating from its inception – the CAP has changed remarkably little.

As Chapter 8 showed, the Commission's latest (Mandate) proposals have, like their predecessors, come to nought. This chapter attempts to assess the various conflicting forces acting upon the CAP for its continued stability or for change. Foremost in most minds is the 'second enlargement' by which is meant the accession of three new members to the Community; one of the three, Greece, has already joined and is in the early stages of adapting to membership. Spain and Portugal are negotiating terms of entry. Such a major expansion of the Community has significant implications for both the agricultural sectors and the economies of member states. As might be expected the Community budget is the focus of attention here. Other forces for change are also evident, including moves towards further integration and the possibility of a trade war and of the Community budget running out of funds. The final part of the chapter is concerned with the choices which face the Community and their relative acceptability to the politicians, together with the likely direction to be taken by the CAP in the next decade.

The second enlargement

This section will examine the accession of Greece as well as the prospective accessions of Spain and Portugal. A brief historical record is necessary before the economic or agricultural implications are considered.

Greece signed an Association Agreement with the EEC on 9 July 1962 with the intention of eventually gaining full membership. One feature of progress towards this end was that Greek agricultural policy was to be gradually harmonized with the CAP, a process for which a period of twelve years was allotted. Developments were abruptly halted by the military dictatorship of 1967–74; then, following the restoration of democracy, Greece applied in 1975 for full membership. Negotiations began the following year, resulting in the signing of an Accession Treaty on 28 May 1979 whereby Greece joined the Community on 1 January 1981.

Portugal and Spain formally applied to join the Community in 1977, on 28 March and 28 July respectively. In 1978 the Commission delivered its opinions on these applications to the Council, recommending early negotiations and co-operation with the applicants to help restructure their economies in preparation for accession. Negotiations with Portugal began in October 1978 and with Spain in February 1979; they have not been completed and the target date for accession – 1 January 1984 – looks increasingly unattainable. The reasons why negotiations are so long and drawn out will shortly become apparent.

Before proceeding to an analysis of the economic implications of this second enlargement it is worth noting the reasons for its occurrence. In the preamble to the Treaty of Rome the founder members declared their intention to pool their resources to 'preserve and strengthen peace and liberty' and called upon other European countries who shared their ideal to join with them. The political motivations for this second enlargement are well recognized. The Commission commented in 1978:

> When Greece, Portugal and Spain, newly emerging as democratic states after a long period of dictatorship, asked to be admitted to the Community, they were making a commitment which is primarily a political one. Their choice is doubly significant, both reflecting the concern of these three new democracies for their own consolidation and protection against the return of dictatorship and constituting an act of faith in a united Europe, which demonstrates that the ideas inspiring the creation of the Community have lost none of their vigour or relevance. (EEC 1978, 6, para. 1)

Although in this quotation the Commission concentrates on the political imperatives of accession for the three Mediterranean countries they see advantages for the existing EEC also. Clearly the Nine are not unaffected by the political and social stability of their immediate neighbours. In addition, the Commission envisages that an enlarged Community will have an enhanced international influence.

Problems of enlargement

Both institutional and economic difficulties will result from such a major expansion of the Community. When progress can occur by unanimous agreement only, the addition of new opinions and interests to every debate must surely slow down decision-making procedures and the process of integration. The Commission has recognized this danger and proposes to meet it by strengthening the institutions and organs of the Community (EEC 1978, 15, para. 48). The obvious implication is that power should be transferred to some extent from the Council of Ministers to the Commission and Parliament; majority voting as envisaged in the Treaty of Rome before the Luxembourg Compromise would presumably become the normal method of reaching agreement.

On the economic front the difficulties of enlargement reflect primarily the disparity in levels of development between the three Mediterranean countries and the existing Community. All three countries have *per capita* GNPs which are lower than that of the previously poorest member, Ireland. Greece and Spain are not far behind Ireland in this respect but Portgal trails by a large margin, having only 60 per cent of Ireland's GNP *per capita*. In an enlarged Community the disparity would be substantially between a rich North European membership (with the exception of Ireland) and a poor Mediterranean South - four members if Italy is included. The seriousness of regional disparities is indicated by comparing *per capita* incomes in the richest and poorest regions. Hamburg is the richest region of the Community, having six times the *per capita* incomes of the West of Ireland and five times that of Calabria. In an enlarged Community Hamburg would have *twelve* times the income level of Vila Real-Branganca in Portugal (ECC 1979b, 10). As might be expected, the poorer regions of the Mediterranean countries have an inadequate economic infrastructure and their provision of social security and public services such as health and education is far below the rest of the Community.

Economic integration in the original Six was considerably facilitated by high rates of economic growth which cushioned the impact of change. At the time of the first enlargement there was still scope for disadvantaged sectors to adjust because opportunities existed elsewhere. In the recession and relative stagnation of the early 1980s the difficulties of adjusting to enlargement are considerably magnified both for the existing Community and for new members. It is against this unfavourable background that the effects of enlargement upon agriculture and the CAP must be viewed.

Enlargement and the CAP

EFFECT ON NEW MEMBERS

New members have to adopt the Community's existing institutions, common policies and laws and adapt to them. Thus the CAP in its entirety must be applied, though gradually during a transitional period. In the case of Greece the Treaty of Accession specifies a five year transition period (except for fresh and processed tomatoes and peaches for which the Community has a surplus and Greece is a major exporter; these have a transition period of seven years). For Spain and Portugal there are greater difficulties and longer transitional periods of seven to ten years are proposed.

Enlarging the Community from nine to twelve will expand agricultural output by a quarter and the agricultural population and area of farmland by a half. In other words, agricultural productivity whether in terms of labour or land is in the Three only half that of the Nine. These unfavourable data reflect the nature of the 'Mediterranean' agriculture which predominates. Arid climates, adverse topography and poor soils lead naturally to a concentration on labour-intensive and low-productivity forms of production such as wine, olive oil and fruit and vegetables. In Greece, for example, a quarter of the utilized agricultural area is on hillsides and an additional one-sixth on mountainsides; agriculture there is very similar to that in the worst part of Italy, the Mezzogiorno, which remains very poor despite the CAP.

The concentration of the Three on Mediterranean products means that their livestock sectors are relatively small and significantly dependent upon imported feeding stuffs. Adoption of the existing CAP would harm these livestock sectors by raising the costs of their feedstuffs and at the same time exposing them to competition from the larger and generally more efficient, livestock sectors of the Community. For the Mediterranean products the situation is very different. The higher CAP prices and intervention system should guarantee significantly enhanced returns to producers whose incomes are much lower than in the Nine, and there is a distinct possibility that the consequence will be very rapidly expanding supplies. Already it is obvious that wine and olive oil will be substantially in surplus; a few fruit and vegetable products will also create problems. As a first example, Greece has already provided the Community with its first dried fruit (currant) mountain. It is generally accepted that the CAP supports temperate products more generously than Mediterranean products despite the relative poverty of the latter regions. Higher support levels for Mediterranean products would exacerbate the severity of surplus problems. There is an obvious conflict between the social needs for supporting Mediterranean products generously and the cost of disposing of the extra surpluses which would be induced.

Estimating the response of producers to higher prices is notoriously difficult. Thus the likely outputs of the Mediterranean area resulting from the application of the CAP as it is at present are not known with any degree of precision. The possibility of more support in recognition of evident social need renders future levels of output even more uncertain. Whatever happens to output it is clear that the CAP would significantly improve agricultural incomes in the Three in general, although their livestock sectors are likely to be disadvantaged.

EFFECT ON THE COMMUNITY

The previous section argued that the application of the CAP to the three Mediterranean countries would increase output to a significant but unknown extent. The consequences of the current outputs of these countries coming under the CAP umbrella indicate the nature of the problems to which CAP-induced expansion would give rise.

On the whole Greek agriculture is complementary with that of the Nine, with Greece importing significant quantities of livestock feeding stuffs, milk products, beef and veal, and exporting mainly fresh and processed fruit and vegetables. Before accession much of this trade was already conducted between the Community and Greece so that the immediate impact of the latter's accession is relatively minor. Nevertheless the Commission has estimated that the accession of Greece would expand FEOGA expenditures by the end of the transitional period by about 600 million ECUs annually (ECC 1980c). This is of about the same order as the net expenditures benefiting Ireland and Denmark.

Portugal has a substantial agricultural trade deficit, importing twice as much as she exports. Whilst half of these exports go to the Nine, imports from the Nine are small. There is, however, little scope for the surpluses of the EEC to be much reduced by the accession of Portugal. This is because the country's major agricultural imports are of animal feeding stuffs, for which the Community also has a deficit. Community surpluses of dairy products would be little affected but those of wheat, sugar and beef would be marginally eased. On the other hand Portugal's major agricultural export, wine, would add to the frequency and severity of surplus problems in this commodity. Food consumption patterns in Portugal could change rapidly if accession significantly accelerated improvements in the standard of living, because incomes are so low initially that about half of the income is spent on food – double the proportion in the Nine. On the other hand consumers have enjoyed prices which have been kept below production costs by subsidies. Whilst it is evidently difficult to do more than guess the extra FEOGA burden which Portugal's accession would impose, on balance one is encouraged to believe that it would be relatively small, both because Portugal is small relative to the Community and because she seems likely to reduce rather than augment existing surpluses.

Enlarging the Community to include Spain presents far greater problems than in the cases of Greece and Portugal. This is partly because Spain is relatively large and would increase by 33 per cent the Community's number of farms, farmers and the farmed area. Spanish agriculture is dominated by crops – mainly vegetables, fruit, cereals, wine and olive oil – in contrast to the Nine where livestock predominate. Because fruit and vegetable production are not supported at all in Spain, and wine and olive oil have lower than CAP prices, there is an expectation of substantial expansion following accession. Spain already has a large surplus in agricultural trade with the Community, the main exports being fresh and processed fruit and vegetables and wine. Application of the CAP would cause two major problems: the Mediterranean regions of France and Italy, already amongst the poorest areas of the Community, would be damaged by lower-cost freely imported Spanish produce. Additionally Community surpluses of some Mediterranean products would be greatly exacerbated. Overall Spain has a considerable deficit in agricultural trade because of her heavy dependence on imported feeding stuffs (like the Nine) for her livestock sector. The latter would find CAP-raised feeding stuff prices difficult to adjust to and would tend to decline, causing extra imports of beef and milk products. Imports of these are already significant and imply a small reduction in existing Community surpluses. There can be no doubt that the CAP would entail major net FEOGA expenditures in Spain although no precise estimates are possible.

EFFECT ON CONSUMERS

Since the CAP would result in higher food prices in the three Mediterranean countries (except for some livestock products), the gains of producers would be at the expense of consumers (and to a less extent taxpayers). Clearly some of the resulting income transfers from consumers to producers would occur within each country but others would be via trade transfers. As was noted in Chapter 6 trade transfers may be inequitable in that income is transferred from poor to richer countries; it was shown there (Table 6.3) that this depends on whether or not a country is a net food importer or exporter. In the Nine, all net food importing countries suffer negative trade transfers, whilst the net food exporters gain. It is notable that this applies markedly to Italy which has much in common with Greece, Spain and Portugal. Since these three countries each have major agricultural trade deficits it follows that the existing CAP will entail major trade transfers from them to the existing net food exporters – *all* of which are richer countries.

COSTS AND BENEFITS

It was noted above that the Commission estimated that the accession of Greece would result in a net cost to the Community's budget as a result of applying the CAP. In the case of Spain, the extra net cost is expected to be much larger – the Commission has stated that the increase in expenditure would exceed the Community's 'own resources' (ECC 1981d). The Commission is currently preparing proposals for a revision of financial arrangements; these proposals, to be presented before the end of June 1983 to the Council, are designed to ensure sufficient extra resources to permit the accessions of Spain and Portugal. How much expansion in the 'own resources' system is necessary for this further enlargement? In the *Report on the Mandate* the Commission noted that in applying the CAP to the acceding Mediterranean areas 'equivalence and equity' should be borne in mind.

'Equivalence' means that, in line with the basic principles of the Treaties, the CAP must apply 'without discrimination to Mediterranean products' (ECC 1981b, 13). In terms of FEOGA a very high proportion of total expenditures so far have been on the northern temperate products and intervention prices for these have been relatively close to target prices, whilst for fruit and vegetables intervention prices are 50–70 per cent only of the desired price levels (Appendix 3.2) Exactly what is implied by 'equal' treatment of Mediterranean produce is not clear, but considerable increases in support expenditures are indicated. Equity in this current context is stated to mean that 'change cannot be allowed to lead to a drop in living standards for those involved' (ECC 1981b, 13). This could be interpreted as a promise that the French and Italian Mediterranean producers would not be harmed by further enlargements. Alternatively it could be that the livestock sectors of the new members would somehow be compensated for higher feeding stuff prices and extra competition. In either or both of these situations additional CAP costs would be involved. Thus it is established that the first element of cost in further enlargement is increased budgetary expenditure – to an unknown extent, but large enough to require an increase in 'own resources' revenues. If the accession of Greece, Spain and Portugal is to bring about a net increase in budgetary expenditures it follows that the three countries should receive more in budgetary receipts than they contribute. But if their economies are to be net beneficiaries of the CAP these positive budgetary transfers will need to exceed the negative trade transfers noted earlier. This does not seem very likely unless the CAP changes very dramatically to favour Mediterranean products.

In any assessment of CAP costs and benefits the criticisms made in the appraisal of the CAP in Chapter 7 should be borne in mind. Basically the enlargement of the Community involves the extension of the CAP to more countries and hence the further misallocation of resources internationally, more trade diversion against the interests of other agricultural exporters and also to their detriment a probable expansion in the dumping of agricultural commodities. Despite these costs and the inequitable international transfers involved the CAP will still not be achieving its main objective of securing fair incomes for the agricultural population. On the contrary, being still a price-based support system the CAP will continue to transfer income from poor consumers to rich producers. This last criticism applies to the three

Mediterranean countries with more force than to the Nine: can it be equitable for Portuguese consumers having such low incomes (that on average half is spent on food) to have to pay higher food prices, the major benefits of which will accrue to richer farmers?

Prospects for change

Within five years of the introduction of the CAP Dr Mansholt told the Council that the price policy alone could not meet the farm income objectives of the Treaty of Rome. Despite his early recognition of the inadequacies of price policy this main element of the CAP has continued virtually unchanged. Now, twenty years after its inception, this remarkable constancy must be explained before the likelihood of future changes can be examined. There are several reasons for inflexiblity built into the system. First, there is the existence of the power of veto; no change can occur without the unanimous agreement of the Council of Ministers. Politicians of different parties do not agree readily, and when different parties and nations are involved difficulties multiply. When the number of EEC members increases the difficulties are further increased. Perhaps the chances of agreement vary inversely with the square of the number of participants (by analogy with the inverse square law of physics). This is of course a very cynical interpretation of the situation, but when the marathon negotiating sessions and package deals involving relatively minor issues are considered it does not seem unfair. Reinforcing the resolves of one or more Ministers to veto changes to the CAP is the fact that the present system favours the national interests of most member states of the Community. In addition, farmers' leaders favour the CAP because of the income transfers which benefit them, and lobby vigorously to make the CAP more generous (to them) rather than to change it in any other way. Finally, the Commission itself, as 'guardian of the Treaties', has gone out of its way to defend the CAP, whereas a more open-minded acknowledgement of its shortcomings could have more effectively sown the seeds of change.

Having noted the amazing lack of change in the CAP and the barriers to change which explain its constancy we now turn to speculate on the sort of circumstances which might presage reform.

FURTHER INTEGRATION

Economic and monetary union, as discussed in Chapter 4, is particularly difficult to achieve during a period of economic instability.

Recent and prospective enlargements make it even more remote than before. So the common prices aspect of the CAP is most unlikely to be restored via a common currency. However, less spectacular but still significant expansions of integration are possible through co-operation.

In 1981 there were two initiatives aimed at revitalizing the Community (see ECC 1982c). The first, sponsored by the German and Italian governments, proposed a number of reforms for promoting European Union and concentrated on areas of political co-operation which were believed to be attainable. The second, in the form of a French memorandum, avoided political references but urged economic co-operation aimed particularly at reducing unemployment. As usual, the opposing approaches of different members towards further integration promise little progress. However, of immediate interest is that both initiatives referred to the Luxembourg Compromise, suggesting that it should be less readily used than at present, with majority voting as provided for in the Treaties becoming of greater importance. This is consistent with the opinion expressed above, that the power of veto is an obstacle to change. Voting procedures are, however, unlikely to become more important, not only because the larger members are determined to guard their national interests as jealously as ever, but also because the smaller members realize that their interests are better protected by powers of veto.

TRADE WARS

On three occasions in the past the Community has proposed to ameliorate its butter surplus problem by taxing the vegetable oils which go into margarine. Each time, these proposals have been dropped because of the threat of retaliation by the major supplier, the USA. As noted in Chapter 7 the Community's agriculture export subsidy system is damaging to the interests of other agricultural exporters. As surpluses expand, as they seem certain to do under the existing CAP (see below), and particularly if further enlargements exacerbate them, third countries will become more severely harmed. Retaliation would probably take the form of curtailed access for industrial products; with unemployment a problem everywhere such measures would be politically popular in the countries concerned. Because the Community relies more heavily upon trade than any other major economic area the results of such retaliations would be catastrophic. This explains the threats of trade wars which were a feature of 1982. It seems probable that the Community has played down the likelihood of such measures on the grounds that her trading partners would not wish to indulge in activities that would weaken the Western Alliance either politically or economically. Nevertheless the threats remain and brinkmanship does not seem advisable when the Community has so much to lose.

An 'all-out' trade war may not be very likely, but trade walls can be constructed brick by brick. It would be sad if the Community, in persisting with a failed agricultural policy, was gradually isolated from the markets of the other developed countries.

BUDGET EXHAUSTION

Most of the Community budget's expenditure is channelled through FEOGA; its revenue is limited by the 'own resources' system to import levies plus a maximum of a 1 per cent rate of VAT. As shown in Table 9.1 the VAT contribution is getting very near to its upper limit. If CAP expenditures increase, the budget would either be unable to fund them or do so at the expense of other policies. Chapter 5 documented the growth of surpluses and disposal costs. Physical surpluses are expected to continue expanding because of the inexorable increase in yields induced through the application of technological advance and encouraged by high support prices. Disposal costs may well grow even more rapidly – they depend on the extent of surpluses and the difference between Community and world market prices (i.e. the export subsidy required) – and world price levels are widely forecast to decline. Unless world food price levels for the major surplus

Table 9.1 Community revenues, 1976–82

	1976	1977	1978	1979	1980	1981	1982
Customs duties	4191.5	4458.9	4390.9	5189.1	5905.8	6366.0	6939.0
Levies (including sugar levies)	1173.3	2137.1	2278.9	2143.5	2002.4	1773.7	2685.1
VAT	2489.8	2557.4	5329.7	7039.8	7354.5	9824.9	11971.1
VAT rate (%)	–	–	0.64	0.79	0.73	0.78	0.91
Own resources*	7854.6	9153.4	11999.5	14372.4	15061.9	17481.9	21595.2

Source: ECC (1981c)
Note: *Including financial contributions

commodities *increase*, the CAP seems likely to become sufficiently expensive to exhaust the budget by the end of 1984. A modest decline in world prices would advance this date, possibly by a year. Since further enlargement is expected to increase net budgetary expenditure there is no reprieve from this quarter.

If budgetary revenues are insufficient to cover expenditures three developments are possible: reform of the CAP to cut costs; the expansion of budgetary revenues; or borrowing to cover the deficit. Each of these major departures will be examined in turn. Of course in the short run a 'temporary' deficit could be financed by 'once-and-for-all' extra contributions.

Cost-reducing CAP reforms.   In the past, whenever the growth of FEOGA expenditures has outpaced 'own resources' the Commission has attempted to follow 'prudent' price policies and has encouraged moderation in the Council of Agriculture Ministers. Indeed it appears that only the prospect of running out of funds has much effect on price decisions, which of course largely determine FEOGA expenditures. Major reforms have so far not been countenanced but lack of money can concentrate minds wonderfully.

The expansion of budgetary revenues.   There is little doubt that most member countries would prefer to see the 'own resources' system given new sources of revenue than suffer any curtailment of CAP expenditures: after all, most would hope to derive net benefits from an expansion as they do from the existing system. Such hopes and expectations would influence the support given to a variety of proposed sources of extra revenues. Perhaps the most obvious extra revenue source is the raising of the VAT limit. At least the additional national contributions would then be proportional to the size of national economies, which superficially makes them appear equitable. However, this would raise UK contributions far more than UK receipts and would therefore probably be vetoed by her – with the support of Germany who would be similarly disadvantaged. Common sense would suggest raising extra revenues from those members responsible for the surpluses which are so expensive to dispose of. This would be the national equivalent of co-responsibility levies which the Commission has attempted to introduce on a commodity basis with little success. Such a system would probably be against the interest of the poorer members of the Community if the surplus levies were at a flat rate. They could, however, easily be at varying rates according to member states' *per capita* GNPs.

Borrowing. Deficit budgeting is the norm for national governments. If the Community was allowed to borrow to finance extra expenditures this would appear to be a simple extension of the principle. It would not be so. By itself it would be an asymmetrical development in that the Community would have spending powers but not taxation powers. This would be a guaranteed recipe for inflation. In conjunction with taxation powers the Community would in reality become a federation. In short, borrowing could only occur as a part of a much larger development and therefore looks politically unlikely at the present time.

COMMISSION PROPOSALS FOR RAISED BUDGETARY CONTRIBUTIONS

Since the above paragraphs were written it has become increasingly obvious that the budget will run out of funds by the end of 1984. As CAP expenditures rise inexorably the Commission has decided that the solution has to lie in extra budget revenues. A variety of suggestions were floated early in 1983, culminating in a new set of Commission proposals published in May. Two reasons for these are put forward: first, that extra resources are necessary for the further development of the Community, particularly its enlargement; second, that a restructuring of the 'own resources' system would solve the UK budget contributions problem.

Extra resources are proposed to be drawn from four sources:

(a) the existing 1 per cent VAT ceiling to be abolished and replaced with a 1.4 per cent ceiling which could be raised further by 0.4 per cent as necessary; each increase would be subject to the unanimous approval of Council and a qualified majority in the European Parliament;

(b) customs duties on imports of European Coal and Steel Community (ECSC) products should accrue to the Community budget instead of, as at present, to national exchequers;

(c) reimbursement of 10 per cent of customs duties and agricultural import levies as collection costs should no longer be automatic;

(d) the power to tax the non-industrial use of energy should be kept in reserve.

Proposals relating to the agricultural section of the budget are more radical. Essentially they are that the CAP should be financed only partially through the 'own resources' system, the remaining finance coming from 'modulated' VAT contributions. The suggested basis of this modulation is each country's share of gross agricultural output, but taking account of relative GNP per head and share of Community 'net operating surplus'. In other words a country would contribute to the cost of the CAP in proportion to its agricultural output except that poorer countries would contribute at a lower rate.

A hypothetical example would illustrate the operation of these proposals. Suppose it was decided that agriculture should account for no more than 30 per cent of the budget instead of the 70 per cent which it now absorbs. Then the expenditure equivalent to 40 per cent would be financed from modulated VAT contributions. These would fall most heavily upon high-income countries with large agricultural surpluses, notably Denmark, France and the Netherlands. German and UK contributions would be correspondingly reduced; they would however remain significant net contributors.

The CAP up to 1990

Interpreting the past and analysing the present may excite controversy but it is difficult to be entirely wrong. Speculating about the future renders the writer a hostage to fortune. Nevertheless some apparently clear portents are worth noting. First, as political imperatives are behind the expected accessions of Portugal and Spain they will doubtless occur, but only well into the second half of the decade. In the summer of 1982 southern French peasants demonstrated their worry that Spanish accession would harm their interests by destroying imported Spanish fruits and vegetables. France requested a Commission study of the consequences of further enlargement on the poorer regions of the Community. Inevitably, and presumably by intention, this will delay accession beyond the January 1984 target date. Other factors are also against early accession, notably the continuing budget problems and the desirability of higher rates of economic growth to facilitate adjustments. The Commission regards a growth rate of 3–4 per cent as necessary.

Finally, the reluctance of Germany and the UK to increase their net contributions to the Community budget 'in the face of expanding

FEOGA costs must be an important factor in forcing some measure of reform. The Commission is almost certain to stick to its demand for more co-responsibility levies since these would both reduce surpluses and their disposal costs as well as consequently pleasing third countries who are upset by the extent of current export subsidies. Opinions are unlikely to change sufficiently to cause a major swing from price to income support, however. In other words the politicians are likely to accept the introduction of co-responsibility levies only to the extent necessitated by budgetary constraints. As a corollary the CAP will continue to dominate the Community budget as it has in the past and so frustrate the development of other Community policies.

In conclusion

This book has attempted to examine the CAP not only in isolation but also in relation to the changes which agriculture undergoes in the course of economic development. Agriculture's major contribution to development, which was noted to be particularly vital in the primary stages, is to release resources to other sectors by improving productivity; an additional significant contribution resulting from growing output is falling real prices for food, which raises living standards and the profitability of the non-agricultural sector. The reallocation of resources released through higher productivity is achieved by their earnings in agriculture declining relative to opportunities in other sectors. It is thus 'natural' for agricultural populations to suffer relative poverty. The small size and often fragmented nature of the majority of European farms render them inefficient as producing units, and so exacerbates the natural tendency towards poverty. The 'farm problem' is seen to have both economic and social dimensions. It is economic in the sense that its causes are partly economic and it is expressed in economic terms as a relatively low income. It is social in that our twentieth-century society regards relatively low incomes for a major sector as unfair.

The CAP was conceived as a policy to enhance economic efficiency and raise agricultural incomes. Indeed the policy as set out in the Treaty of Rome implied that the latter objective could be achieved as a consequence of improving efficiency. Yet the policy instruments chosen militated against efficiency. Agricultural prices were raised by tariff barriers, which reduced imports, and by export subsidies designed to dump surpluses on the world market. Such measures enabled inefficient producers to survive; they and other resources were retained in agriculture although they might (before the present recession) have found more productive employment elsewhere.

This analysis has pointed out that improving agricultural productivity has been a major driving force in economic change down the centuries. The pace of productivity increases has been faster in this than in any previous century and has accelerated dramatically since the introduction of the CAP. This coincidence has been most unfortunate: at the time when the application of scientific advances was raising output at unprecedented rates the CAP guaranteed high prices for all the food which European farmers could produce – without limit! High food prices thus stimulated supplies, but demand could not increase much because the Community's population was already well fed. Rapidly expanding food surpluses have been the consequence of this situation. To prevent such surpluses causing the collapse of food prices within the Community they have been purchased and dumped on world markets.

The costs of the CAP have been discussed in earlier chapters. Four major elements of cost were identified from the point of view of the Community as a whole. First there is a misallocation of resources within the Community resulting from protecting agriculture more generously than other industries, which might have been able to use some of the resources retained in agriculture more profitably. Second, there is a misallocation of resources internationally; in brief, much food has been produced within the Community which could have been imported much more cheaply. Third, it does not make a lot of sense to produce surpluses to sell at a loss to the Russians, or to anyone else. It is this third item of cost which has excited most attention because it involves cash subsidies which are very large and well publicized as they appear in the Community's budget. The fourth element of cost is substantially larger but almost neglected. It is the transfer of income from consumers to producers which artificially high prices cause. Such transfers are not obvious, but these costs exceed those appearing in the budget.

In the early days of the Community the CAP was perceived as a move towards the integration of its member states; it was the first major common policy. There is no doubt that in the past decade it has become a force for disintegration. This is true in a negative sense in that the CAP's mammoth share of the budget has left few resources available for the development of other common policies. Similarly, through its cost and lack of success the CAP is slowing the integration process by delaying the further enlargement of the Community to include Portugal and Spain. Finally, the CAP is a positive force towards disintegration because of the ill-feeling which it generates between member states. As discussed in Chapter 6, the CAP results in very large budgetary and trade transfers between member states; in many instances these transfers are from poor to richer member states. An annual battle between the UK and the other members over a budget refund is the most notable example of the nationalistic antagonisms which such situations arouse. Yet nationalism was the acknowledged evil against which the Community was particularly aimed.

The CAP has been shown to be extremely expensive from almost every possible viewpoint, and to have a variety of other blemishes also; but has it achieved its objectives? This question was examined in Chapter 7 and with one exception – the achievement of stable prices – the answer was a resounding *no*. Judged by the primary objective of raising agricultural incomes to levels similar to those of the non-agricultural sector, the CAP has been a dismal failure. Agricultural incomes are on average approximately half those of the rest of the economy, just as they were when the Community began in 1958. Within agriculture the distribution of incomes is very disparate, and it is widely acknowledged – even by the Commission – that the CAP has tended to exacerbate such disparity: the CAP has benefited the larger, richer farmers in the more prosperous regions rather than the poor 'peasant' farmers whose poverty it is supposed to ameliorate. This failure of the CAP to redistribute incomes on a more equitable basis is comprehensive, indeed perverse, for its redistribution has largely been from poor countries to richer countries and from poor consumers to richer farmers.

Why has the CAP achieved so little at such enormous cost? Because it has been based on a highly protective system which raises prices to the consumer and concomitantly rewards farmers in proportion to output (and hence size and wealth) rather than need. At least this is the usual economic judgement; the real answer is more fundamental: the basic problem of the CAP is that it attempts to defy the underlying forces of economic development. These inexorably cause agricultural prices and resource earnings to fall in relative terms, and in trying to reverse this tide the CAP has induced a flood of surpluses.

If the CAP continues as it is at present the costs of surplus disposal will bankrupt the Community sometime between the autumn of 1983 and the end of 1984 unless world prices unexpectedly reverse their current downward trend. This unpleasant possibility could be precipitated earlier by a trade war with the USA. Reform or extra finance are the two alternatives to bankruptcy. No significant reform of the CAP has been made since its inception and none appears likely in the immediate future. The Commission is calling for extra budgetary resources both to finance current commitments and to permit the enlargement of the Community. Germany and the UK would be foolish to agree to any change which does not radically change the system of financing the CAP so that the costs of surplus disposal fall more than at present on those who produce them. The history of the CAP contains no evidence which suggests that either the Commission or the politicians of member states have the understanding, imagination or courage to devise or adopt essential reforms. It is therefore probable that the imminent prospect of budgetary exhaustion will be removed via extra budgetary contributions. This new agreement will be a typical package deal which will be announced as a great step forward by the Community; it will, as always, promise far-reaching reforms of the CAP. The author expects (with a sense of regret and frustration) that, as with all such promises made in the past, the CAP will be changed very little.

References

Agra Europe (various), London, Agra Europe Ltd.

Blancus, P. (1978) 'The Common Agricultural Policy and the balance of payments of the EEC member countries', *Banca Nationale del Lavoro - Quarterly Review*, 127, 355–70.

Buckwell, A. E., Harvey, D. R., Thompson, K. T. and Parton, K. A. (1982) *The Costs of the Common Agricultural Policy*, London, Croom Helm.

Butterwick, M. and Rolfe, E. N. (1968) *Food, Farming and the Common Market*, Oxford, Oxford University Press.

ECC (European Communities Commission)

(1968) *Memorandum sur la réforme de l'agriculture dans la Communauté Economique Européenne*, COM (68) 1000, Luxembourg (The Mansholt Plan).

(1970) *Réforme de l'agriculture (propositions de la commission au Conseil)*, COM (70) 500 EEC, Brussels.

(1972a) *Modernisation of Farms*, Directive 72/159/EEC.

(1972b) *Cessation of Farming and the Reallocation of Agricultural Land for Structural Improvement*, Directive 72/160/EEC.

(1972c) *Provision of Socio-economic Guidance*, Directive 72/161/EEC.

(1975a) *Mountain and Hill Farming and Farming in Certain Less-favoured Areas*, Directive 75/268/EEC.

(1975b) *The Common Market and the Common Good*, Luxembourg.

(1978) *Bulletin of the European Communities, Supplement 1/78*, Luxembourg.

(1979a) *The Agricultural Policy of the European Community*, European Documentation Series, Luxembourg.

(1979b) *The Second Enlargement*, European Documentation Series, Luxembourg.

(1980a) *Reflections on the Common Agricultural Policy*, Luxembourg.

(1980b) *The Agricultural Situation in the Community 1980*, Luxembourg.

(1980c) 'The agricultural aspects of the enlargement of the Community – Greece', *Green Europe 173*, Luxembourg.

(1980d) *Bulletin EC*, 5, 9.

(1981a) 'A new common structure policy', *Green Europe 181*, Luxembourg.

(1981b) *Report on the Mandate* (Report from the Commission of the European Communities to the Council pursuant to the Mandate of 30 May 1980), *Bulletin EC*, Supplement 1/81.

(1981c) *The Agricultural Situation in the Community 1981*, Luxembourg.

(1981d) 'The agricultural aspects of the enlargement of the Community – Spain', *Green Europe 174*, Luxembourg.

(1982a) *The Agricultural Situation in the Community 1982*, Luxembourg.

(1982b) 'Guidelines for European Agriculture', in ECC, *A New Impetus for the Common Policies*, Luxembourg.

(1982c) *Background Report*, ISEC/B26/82, Luxembourg.

(1982d) *Bulletin EC*, 7/8.

HM Government

(1971) *The United Kingdom and the European Communities*, Cmnd 4715, London, HMSO.

(1974) *Renegotiation of the Terms of Entry into the EEC*, Cmnd 5593, London, HMSO.

(1975) *Britain's New Deal in Europe*, London, HMSO. (Booklet distributed on behalf of the Government to every household in the UK recommending a 'yes' vote in the Community membership referendum.)

House of Lords Select Committee on the European Communities

(1980) *The Common Agricultural Policy*, 32nd Report, Session 1979–80, HL 156, London, HMSO.

(1981) *The Common Agricultural Policy*, 19th Report, Session 1979–80, HL 126, London, HMSO.

(1982a) *Agricultural Trade Policy*, 2nd Report, Session 1981–2, HL 29, London, HMSO.

(1982b) *State Aids to Agriculture*, 7th Report, Session 1981–2, HL 90, London, HMSO.

Johnson, H. G. (1958) 'The gains from freer trade: an estimate', *Manchester School*, March, 247–55.

Josling, T. E. (1973) 'The reform of the CAP', in Evans, D. (ed.) *Britain in the EEC*, London, Gollancz.

Koester, V. (1978) *The CAP and Our Food*, Wye, CEAS, Wye College.

Malgren, H. B. and Scheckty, D. L. (1969) 'Technology and neo-mercantilism in international agricultural trade'. *American Journal of Agricultural Economics (AJAE)*, December, 1326.

Mansholt, S. (1979) *An Interview on the CAP*, Stowmarket, The Soil Association.

Marsh, J. (1977) *UK Agricultural Policy within the EEC*, Reading, CAS, University of Reading.

Marsh, J. and Ritson, C. (1971) *Agricultural Policy and the Common Market*, London, Chatham House-PEP.

Metcalf, D. (1969) *The Economics of Agriculture*, Harmondsworth, Penguin.

Milk Marketing Board (annually) *EEC Dairy Facts and Figures*.

Ministry of Agriculture, Paris (1969) *Rapport général de la commission sur l'avenir à long terme de l'agriculture francais présidée par M. le doyen Georges Vedel*, Paris.

Morris, C. N. (1980) *The Common Agricultural Policy*, London, Institute of Fiscal Studies.

OECD (Organization for Economic Co-operation and Development) (1973) *Agricultural Policy in Greece*, Paris.
(1974a) *Agricultural Policy in Spain*, Paris.
(1974b) *Agricultural Policy in the EEC*, Paris.
(1975) *Agricultural Policy in Portugal*, Paris.

Pearce, J. (1981) *The Common Agricultural Policy*, London, Routledge & Kegan Paul.

Rickard, R. C. (1970) 'Structural policies for agriculture in the EEC', *Journal of Agricultural Economics (JAE)* XXI, 3, 407–29.

Roberts, I. and Tie, G. (1982) 'The emergence of the EEC as a net exporter of grain', *Quarterly Review of the Rural Economy 4*, 4, 295–304.

Rollo, J. M. C. and Warwick, K. S. (1979) *The CAP and Resource Flows among EEC Member States*, Government Service Working Paper No. 27, London, HMSO.

Schultz, T. W. (1954) *The Economic Organisation of Agriculture*, New York, McGraw-Hill.

Statistical Office of the European Communities
(1980) *Land Use and Production 1955-79*, Brussels.

(1982) *Eurostat Revue 1971-80*, Brussels.

Strasser, D. (1980) *The Finances of Europe*, Luxembourg, European Communities.

Swann, D. (1978) *The Economics of the Common Market*, 4th edn, Harmondsworth, Penguin.

Warley, T. K. (1967) *Agriculture: the Cost of Joining the Common Market*, London, Chatham House-PEP.

Welmesfelder, W. (1960) 'The short-run effects of the lowering of import duties in Germany', *Economic Journal*, March, 94–104.

Index

Printed in the United States
by Baker & Taylor Publisher Services

Printed in the United States
by Baker & Taylor Publisher Services